A CHOICE NOT AN ECHO

Phyllis Schlafly

PERE MARQUETTE PRESS

P. O. Box 316   Alton, Illinois

First Edition .... May 1964
600,000 copies
Second Edition .... June 1964
1,000,000 copies
Third Edition .... August 1964

The first edition of A CHOICE NOT AN ECHO, published May 1, 1964, correctly predicted who would be the kingmakers' candidates at the 1964 Republican National Convention, and foretold the tactics they would use in their efforts to stop Barry Goldwater.

This revised (third) edition tells what happened in San Francisco and warns against the kingmakers' continuing propaganda against Senator Goldwater.

Printed in the United States of America

Table of Contents

"A CHOICE NOT AN ECHO made a major contribution to the victory of Senator Goldwater at the Republican Convention in San Francisco. If read by enough people, I am confident it will help elect him to the Presidency and thus preserve our heritage of freedom and decency in human relationships . . . It is absolutely the finest collection of evidence I have seen."
— General A. C. Wedemeyer, U. S. Army (Ret.)

"Phyllis Schlafly has written the book of the year . . . Although the book is written primarily to alert Republican voters, it will be of equal interest to Democratic voters."
— Major General Thomas A. Lane, U. S. Army (Ret.)

"The distribution of a half-million copies of A CHOICE NOT AN ECHO in California prior to the June 2 primary was a major factor in bringing victory to Barry Goldwater against the terrific assault of the press, the pollsters and the paid political workers of the opposition."
— Gardiner Johnson, Republican National Committeeman for California

"Mrs. Schlafly gave us a tool when we needed it most. It was a magic wand that really converted people to Barry Goldwater."
— Mrs. Edgar Eisenhower

Chapter One

The Billion Dollar Robberies

Newspapers still headline stories about the $7 million London train robbery of 1963 and the earlier $1.2 million Brink's robbery in 1950 in Boston. Yet the press is strangely silent about the $13 billion robbery of 1940, the $98 billion robbery of 1944, the $39 billion robbery of 1948, or the $81 billion robbery of 1960.

In each of those years the American people were robbed of their constitutional birthright to a Presidential choice. At stake was control of the annual Federal spending which rose from $13 billion in 1941 to $100 billion in 1964.

The advance planning and sense stimuli employed to capture a $10 million cigarette or soap market are nothing compared to the brainwashing and propaganda blitzes used to insure control of the largest cash market in the world: the Executive Branch of the United States Government.

Most Americans think the next president of the United States will be selected on the first Tuesday after the first Monday in November 1964 when we go to the polls to vote. Most Americans think they will vote for a candidate who has been selected in their Party's political convention by Delegates who voted their honest convictions and chose the man best qualified to lead their Party to victory. This may be what is taught in the schoolbooks, but this ideal is frequently contrary to political reality.

From 1936 through 1960 the Republican presidential nominee was selected by a small group of secret kingmakers who are the most powerful opinion makers in the world. They dictated the choice of the Republican presidential nominee just as completely as the Paris dressmakers control the length of women's skirts. In the 1940's when the decree went out from Paris that all women's skirts should be only fourteen inches off the floor, every family budget in the United States was unbalanced in a frantic effort to achieve the "new look".

Each fall 66 million American women don't spontaneously decide their dresses should be an inch or two shorter, or longer, than last year. Like sheep, they bow to the wishes of a select clique of couturiers whom they have never seen, and whose names they may not even know.

It is easy to predict that, when skirts get about as short as they can possibly go, a Paris edict will be handed down again, and otherwise-sensible American women, even when they cannot afford such extravagance, will throw or give away perfectly good dresses in order to buy new ones which will meet the fashion dictates of a half dozen dressmakers in Paris.

In the same way, a few secret kingmakers based in New York selected every Republican presidential nominee from 1936 through 1960, and successfully forced their choice on a free country where there are more than 34 million Republican voters. Fantastic? In this book, we will examine the record and see how they did it. The strategy of politics, like an iceberg, is eight-ninths under the surface.

But, first, let us look at the issues of the 1964 election year.

Chapter Two

Who's Looney Now?

Every newspaper, every newscast on radio and television, every statement of public officials — testifies to the numerous important political issues of the 1964 campaign year.

I. DEFEATS AROUND THE WORLD. A map of the world reveals the collapse of American foreign policy everywhere.

LAOS, as a result of the troika coalition government forced upon our friends by Ambassador Averell Harriman, is now under Communist control. This is in spite of the fact that Laos received more United States foreign aid per capita than any nation in the world, and was the scene of the dedicated private charity of the heroic Dr. Tom Dooley.

VIET NAM, slipping fast into Communist clutches, is now embroiled in a bloody war in which American boys are fighting and dying with little hope, under the policies of the present Administration, of winning.

CAMBODIA, which has received generous amounts of foreign aid, has ordered our diplomatic representatives out of the country.

PAKISTAN and INDIA are angry at us for the military aid we have given the other.

GREECE, the country we saved from Communism under the Greek-Turkish Aid Program, has been the scene of rampaging anti-American mobs which burn President Johnson in effigy.

FRANCE and ENGLAND, our old friends, have broken with American policy, recognized Red China, and told President Johnson they will trade with Cuba and the Soviet Union whether we like it or not.

We have lost the friendship of our NATO ally PORTUGAL because our State Department sided with Portugal's enemies when they seized Goa and attempted to seize Angola.

We have lost the friendship of our NATO ally the NETHERLANDS because the Democratic policy under Bobby Kennedy encouraged Sukarno to steal Dutch New Guinea.

The CONGO, as a direct result of the coalition policy forced upon it by the Democratic State Department through the UN, is in utter chaos, with gangs of savages terrorizing and killing missionaries and other white people.

In ALGERIA, Communist Ben Bella, who was welcomed to America by the Democratic Administration with a 21-gun salute on the White House lawn, is building a Castro-like state.

In 1960 the Democratic presidential and vice presidential candidates made a major issue of our "image" abroad. They promised to increase respect for America among foreign countries. Four years later, Americans are more hated by more people than ever in our history. In many countries on every continent, the American Flag

is being dragged down, American property is
being confiscated, American citizens are being
seized and humiliated.

II. CASTRO AND CUBA. After the Bay
of Pigs invasion that turned into a triumph for
Castro, and after the phony "blockade" of October 1962 that turned into a triumph for Khrushchev, the problem of Cuba is still with us. The
Johnson Administration apparently has no plans
for doing anything to solve it. No one knows
how many Soviet missiles are still in Cuba, aimed
at targets in the United States. No one knows
how many Soviet troops and "technicians" are
directing military operations in Cuba and train-
ing Latin Americans for subversion.

We do have documented evidence that Castro
is a fountainhead for subversion in Panama,
Venezuela, throughout Latin America, and all
the way to Zanzibar.

On January 17, 1964, Khrushchev repeated his
claim that he had moved missiles out of Cuba
only in return for a United States pledge not to
invade that island. He said:

> "We got a pledge that there will be no
> invasion of Cuba."[1]

Not a single responsible official of the Johnson Administration denied Khrushchev's boast.
The American people can only conclude that the
Democrats in fact did make such a pledge, and
that the Johnson Administration intends to fulfill it. Worse, the Democrats not only pledged
no invasion of Cuba by the United States, but

they are using our Navy and Coast Guard to prevent the Cuban Freedom Fighters from conducting guerrilla warfare against Castro.

The slogan of the Johnson Administration seems to be:

> "Don't worry about the Reds — they are
> still 90 miles away!"

How long can we tolerate this Communist base in Cuba, with Castro insulting and harassing us, spreading his infection throughout the Western Hemisphere giving the Soviets the opportunity to zero in their missiles on American cities?

III. SURVIVAL. Hitler told the world his plans for world conquest in MEIN KAMPF. Western leaders refused either to read or to believe his clear design for aggression. The Communists also have laid out their blueprint for world conquest.

On November 18, 1956, Khrushchev told Western diplomats at a Moscow reception:

> "Whether you like it or not history is on
> our side. We will bury you."[2]

Each year Khrushchev has accelerated his time-table. On July 6, 1960 in Kaprun, Austria, he said:

> "In the short time I still have to live, I
> would like to see the day when the Communist flag flies over the whole world."[3]

On January 17, 1961, Khrushchev predicted that the "victory of world Communism is no longer far off."[4] In Bucharest, Romania on July 19, 1962, Khrushchev boasted:

> "I am convinced that tomorrow the Red
> flag will fly over the United States. But,
> we will not fly the flag. The American
> people will hoist it themselves."[5]

Khrushchev has tested and exploded super hydrogen bombs many megatons more powerful than ours. Communism controls one-fourth of the earth's land surface and one-third of its population. In the last three years, our enemy has acquired missile and submarine bases in Africa and in the Western Hemisphere.

The most important national problem is the survival of American freedom and independence in the face of the Communist threat. Instead of promising to protect our Republic from the greatest threat in our history, the response of the present Democratic Administration is summed up in three policy documents:

1)*State Department Publication* 7277 entitled "Freedom From War", which lays out the official policy of the present administration to abolish our Army, our Navy, our Air Force and our nuclear weapons, and make us subject to a "United Nations Peace Force."[6]

2) *The Rostow Report,* a master plan on foreign policy and disarmament authored by Walt W. Rostow, chairman of the State Department's Policy Planning Board.[7] The thesis of the Rostow Report is that the Communists are "mellowing", that we must abandon our first-strike weapons, that we must not seek victory of the United

States over the Soviet Union or of capitalism over Communism, that we must never give any encouragement to revolts behind the Iron Curtain, that we should deny U. S. foreign aid to countries in order to force them into coalition governments with the Communists as was done in Laos, that we must work toward general and complete disarmament, and that the Administration should embark on a systematic publicity campaign in order to sell Congress and the American people on disarmament. These are now the policies of the Johnson Administration.

3) *The Phoenix Report,* prepared for the U.S. Arms Control and Disarmament Agency.[8] The thesis of the Phoenix Report is that we should abandon the old objectives of "containment" and "coexistence" in favor of a "detente" or "interdependence" between the U.S. and the Soviet Union, that we should have only parity of military force with the USSR, that the President should trick the American people into unilateral disarmament by a tax cut which would force a decrease in spending on national defense, and that we should seriously consider "unification" of the U.S. and the USSR.

The American people would never vote for State Department Publication 7277, the Rostow Report or the Phoenix Report if given a chance at the polls! The big question is, can the Johnson Administration with help of the New York kingmakers put these policies into effect without the American people realizing it until it is too late?

IV. THE PANAMA CANAL. In early January 1964, Communist-led mobs rioted in Panama and marched on our Panama Canal. The role of Red agents trained by Castro has been confirmed by our Secretaries of State and the Army.[9] Since Castro's unsuccessful invasion of Panama in 1959, he has built up a cadre of 700 hardcore agents operating inside Panama.[10]

After the rioting Khrushchev bellowed:

> "Get out before it is too late, before you are chucked out . . . We side with the people of Panama."[11]

The Communist apparatus throughout the world echoed the Red line.

What did the Johnson Administration do? Did LBJ announce that America's vital interests in the Panama Canal would be defended? Did he tell the world that the Panama Canal is a lawfully-purchased American territory, just like the Louisiana Purchase and Alaska, and that we have been more than generous with the Panamanians?

No, LBJ said on January 23 that the U.S. is willing to engage in "reconsideration of all issues" between the U.S. and Panama and on March 21 to consider "every problem which the Panamanian government wishes to raise."

Americans should beware of the Johnson-Rusk State Department entering into negotiations about the Panama Canal. Based on past history, it looks as though the State Department is soft-

ening public opinion for another giveaway of free-world rights and territory that will rank with the tragic Roosevelt and Truman concessions at Teheran, Yalta and Potsdam.

V. COMMUNIST AGENTS IN THE STATE DEPARTMENT AND THE CIA. State Department Security Officer Scott McLeod listed 648 State Department employees as having had Communist activities and associations and 94 as perverts. His successor Otto F. Otepka was fired by Dean Rusk for cooperating with the Senate Internal Security Subcommittee. Top Soviet secret police defectors Yuri Nossenko and Michael Goleniewski have described the Red penetration of our State Department and CIA.[12] Congressman Michael Feighan quotes Goleniewski as saying that, when he went to be debriefed by high CIA officials, he found "one of my own agents sitting in front of me."[13] President Johnson and Dean Rusk are trying to sweep these facts under the rug for fear of another Alger Hiss scandal in an election year.

VI. AMERICAN JETS SHOT DOWN BY THE SOVIETS. On January 28, 1964 the Russians shot down an unarmed American trainer plane that had wandered over East Germany during a storm. The crew of three was killed. After issuing a perfunctory protest, the next day the State Department announced "the incident is closed".

On March 10 the Communists shot down another American plane. Western radar watchers

report there have been 95 Red violations of
Western air space in the last two years. Yet no
Red plane has ever been shot down, or even shot
at, by the West.

How long will the Communists continue to
kill Americans and humiliate us before the world?
The Johnson Administration has no answer.

VII. THE OPPENHEIMER AWARD. One
of Johnson's first acts after becoming President
was personally to present the Enrico Fermi
Award, which carries with it a tax free purse of
$50,000, to J. Robert Oppenheimer.

When anyone tries to say there is no dif-
ference between Republicans and Democrats,
remember this case of J. Robert Oppenheimer.
The Eisenhower Administration, with Lewis
Strauss as Chairman of the Atomic Energy
Commission, revoked Oppenheimer's security
clearance. Some of the evidence against Oppen-
heimer was summarized by William L. Borden,
Executive Director of the Congressional Joint
Committee on Atomic Energy, who testified that
J. Robert Oppenheimer

> "was contributing substantial monthly sums
> to the Communist Party; . . . his wife and
> younger brother were Communists; . . . he
> had at least one Communist mistress . . .
> he was responsible for employing a num-
> ber of Communists . . . at wartime Los
> Alamos . . ."[14]

Oppenheimer admitted that he deliberately told
a "tissue of lies" to a security officer of the U.S.
Army about a contact with him attempted by a

Soviet agent.

This is the man whom President Johnson personally presented with the Fermi award and $50,000. Not a single Republican attended the presentation ceremony at the White House.

VIII. THE EDMUND WILSON AWARD.

On December 6, 1963 President Johnson presented the Presidential Medal of Freedom to Edmund Wilson. This is the highest award that any civilian can receive in peacetime. Edmund Wilson's name is unknown to most Americans, so it is appropriate to tell who he is.

He has had four wives.

He is the author of a book so immoral that, even under our contemporary standards, its sale had to be stopped in many places. The banning of his book in New York State was even upheld by the United States Supreme Court.[15]

By his own admission, Edmund Wilson voted the Communist ticket in 1932, and the Socialist ticket in every other election when Norman Thomas was a candidate.

Edmund Wilson revealed his lack of patriotism in these words from his latest book:

> "I have finally come to feel that this country, whether or not I continue to live in it, is no longer any place for me."[16]

Finally, he did not file any income tax return for nine years. He wrote a book bragging about it called THE COLD WAR AND THE INCOME TAX.

Yet, one of LBJ's first acts as President was

to present a Medal of Freedom to Edmund Wilson.

Failing to file any income tax return is a favorite failing of Democrat liberals. One of the most prominent Democrats of our time, Alben Barkley, failed to file any income tax return for years, including all the time he was Vice President and some of the years he was Majority Leader of the Senate, steering Democrat tax increases through Congress.

Another prominent Democrat liberal who failed to file any income tax return for five years, although his income was more than $60,000 each year, was Dean James Landis, business associate and close personal friend of Joseph P. Kennedy. When the Government finally caught up with him, do you think he received the sentence that any ordinary citizen would receive? Certainly not. He was given a 30-day rest in the finest suite at the most luxurious hospital in New York.[17] Dean Landis held many high government positions under both the New Deal and the New Frontier. Under the Kennedy Administration, which was part of the time he failed to file any income tax returns, he was chairman of a special commission to draw up a code of ethics for Government employees.

IX. THE BOBBY BAKER CASE. President Lyndon Johnson admitted that he accepted from his friend and protege, Bobby Baker, a hi-fi set that cost $585 wholesale and was worth $800-

900 retail. Several years ago Sherman Adams was forced to resign when it was discovered that he had accepted a vicuna coat from Bernard Goldfine. Should not the same principle be applied to LBJ?

Bobby Baker, by his own sworn statement, rose from a net worth of $11,000 to $2,100,000 — while he held a full time Government job obtained for him by Lyndon Johnson. He received a $100,000 loan from a bank which did not even inquire what his income was. He received a $54,000 loan from the Small Business Administration under circumstances that no one else would have received a loan.

When called to testify before a Senate Committee, Bobby Baker took the Fifth Amendment many times, as did his secretary whom he falsely listed as his "cousin" in order to evade a District of Columbia zoning regulation.

The public reacted vigorously in the election of 1952 against the mink coats and the deep freezes of the Truman Administration. These were minor compared to the insider deals and the extremely valuable favors given to the LBJ radio and television stations by Democratic officeholders.

* * * * * *

A popular story of a generation ago concerned an escapee from a nuthouse who, upon learning that the farmers had been ordered by the New Deal to plow under every third row of cotton and to destroy surplus wheat and oranges, exclaimed "Who's looney now?"

There are a number of people in Washington today to whom this expression could apply. Here are a few of the many inconsistencies and contradictions in the policies of the present Administration.

While LBJ is turning out the lights in the White House to save a few dollars — he is also turning out the lights of freedom all over the world by spending $44 million on wheat for the Communist slavemasters. Who's looney now?

The Johnson Administration is sending American boys 9,000 miles away to fight and die against the Communists in Viet Nam — but the Johnson Administration won't do anything at all about the Communists only 90 miles away in Cuba. Who's looney now?

The Johnson Administration is spending $6 billion per year to put a man on the moon — and incidentally the space center in Texas is the chief beneficiary of this boondoggle — but the Johnson Administration won't send a man to Guantanamo to turn on the water. Who's looney now?

The Democrat Administration had a pretended economy drive and closed our 45 missile bases in Turkey and Italy, cancelled the Skybolt missile, the RS-70 reconnaissance strike bomber, and the Nike-Zeus anti-missile-missile because they are too expensive — but they tell us we can't cut a nickel out of foreign aid to the pro-Communist dictators such as Tito and Nkrumah. Who's looney now?

The Democrat Administration refused to see the anti-Communist Madame Nhu and, while she was visiting in America, gave the green light to her enemies to go ahead and murder her husband[18] — but on the other hand, the Democrat Administration lavished millions of dollars of American aid and every possible hospitality on the pro-Communist dictator Sukarno, providing him with three call girls (a Latin type, an American type, and a Nordic type) as his travelling companions in violation of the Mann Act.[19] Who's looney now?

When the Communists rioted at the Panama Canal, and when the Soviets shot down an American plane killing the crew, LBJ did nothing — but President Johnson went into emergency action and kept Congress in session on Christmas Eve in order to get approval to sell 64 million bushels of wheat to the Communists at a price cheaper than Americans pay. Who's looney now?

Many Democrats such as Senators Lausche, Dodd and Thurmond and their millions of supporters do not want to bury the issues of using U.S. tax collections to crush anti-Communists in Katanga and Viet Nam, and to subsidize the sale and transportation of wheat to our enemies. On March 14, 1964, Senator Lausche told Dean Rusk that such trade "is tantamount to telling the world we've gone to bed with the Communists." And Senator Dodd rejected the attempted distinction Rusk and Under Secretary of State Ball made between Yugoslavia and Poland and other Communist nations, saying: "All of us recognize they're on that side and not on our side."

Because of our two-party system, these anti-Communist Democrats are subject to direct and indirect restrictions in their freedom to criticize the Johnson Administration. But these anti-Communist Democrats hope and pray Republicans will fulfill the chief responsibility of the opposition party — which is to oppose the present Administration.

Chapter Three

Republicans Can't Lose—Unless

With all these issues — issues which are vital to the survival and security of America — issues for which Republicans have the facts and arguments on their side — it looks as though there is no way Republicans can possibly lose *so long as we have a presidential candidate who campaigns on the issues*.

But, the reader may ask, isn't that what a presidential nominee is supposed to do — campaign on the issues? Yes, but let us look at the record and see what actually happened in past campaigns.

In 1940 the Republican candidate, Wendell Willkie, did not campaign on the chief issue of that year, which was Roosevelt's policy of consenting to Stalin's invasions of Poland, Finland, Latvia, Lithuania and Estonia — while committing American boys to fight Hitler. When Willkie finally made a few statements on this subject late in the campaign, voters instinctively knew his peace pledges were just "campaign oratory." The second major issue, Roosevelt's violation of the tradition against a third term, was given only superficial mention by Willkie.[1]

In 1944, candidate Thomas Dewey never mentioned the best issue Republicans had that year — how the Roosevelt Administration manipulated and invited the disaster at Pearl Harbor by the policy described by Roosevelt's Secretary of War as "how we should maneuver the Japs into the position of firing the first shot without allowing too much danger to ourselves." At the personal request of General George Marshall (who was criticized by the Army Pearl Harbor Board for failing to warn the Pearl Harbor command after receiving the decoded Jap war messages), Dewey reneged on Republican plans to make the Pearl Harbor disaster a campaign issue. Dewey lost that year and a whole generation of Americans has grown up ignorant of how World War II began.

In 1948, Republican candidates Thomas Dewey and Earl Warren did not campaign on the major issue of that year, which was Communist infiltration in Government. The exposure of Alger Hiss, Harry Dexter White and other Communists in high Government positions had given Republicans their best issue — but Dewey and Warren did not discuss it. By his "Little Sir Echo" campaign, Dewey snatched defeat from the jaws of victory.

In 1952 Republicans were fortunate to have a candidate, Dwight Eisenhower, who squarely faced the issues of that year and approved a hard-hitting campaign. "Corruption, Communism and Korea" were the three dramatic, obvious, winning issues that elected Eisenhower with 55 per cent of the popular vote and won a Republican majority in Congress.

In 1956 Republicans again offered the voters a clearcut choice over the liberalism of Adlai Stevenson.

In 1960, Republican candidate Richard Nixon pulled his punches, thereby bringing about another defeat. He never mentioned what informed Republicans considered his best issue: the Senate record of Kennedy and Johnson, including Kennedy's sponsorship of legislation helpful to the Communists, namely, the repeal of the loyalty oath provision in the National Defense Education Act, and the repeal of the Battle Act provision which prohibited the sending of strategic materials to Iron Curtain countries, and Johnson's killing of anti-Communist legislation such as the bill to restore to the states the right to punish subversion. In the first Nixon-Kennedy television debate (which had the largest audience of all) Kennedy said his objective was "to pick up where FDR left off." Nixon could have told voters where FDR actually left off — at Yalta. But he yielded his right to reply, and lost ground from then until November.

How did it happen that, in four major Presidential campaigns, Republicans were maneuvered into nominating candidates who did not campaign on the major issues?

It wasn't any accident. It was planned that way. In each of their losing presidential years, a small group of secret kingmakers, using hidden persuaders and psychological warfare techniques, manipulated the Republican National Convention to nominate candidates who would sidestep or suppress the key issues.

The kingmakers and their propaganda apparatus have launched a series of false slogans designed to mask the failure of their candidates to debate the major issues. Some of these are the following: "Politics should stop at the water's edge." "We must unite behind our President who has sole power in the field of foreign affairs." "Foreign policy should be bipartisan." In the words of one great Republican leader, "Bipartisanship is just a $5 word for . . . a two-bit word, 'me-tooism'."[2]

The real motive behind these false and dangerous slogans is that the secret kingmakers do not want the New Deal-New Frontier foreign policy — in which they have a vested interest — debated, investigated, or submitted to the voters. Republicans should recognize the truth of the testament handed down by Senator Robert A. Taft shortly before his death:

> "We cannot clean up the mess in Washington, balance the budget, reduce taxes, check creeping Socialism, tell what is muscle or fat in our sprawling rearmament programs, purge subversives from our State Department, unless we come to grips with our foreign policy, upon which all other policies depend."

Politics makes strange bedfellows. The secret kingmakers have made common cause with the Democrats who had everything to gain and nothing to lose if the Republicans made a weak cam-

paign.

One of the favorite tricks of the Democrats is to try to get the Republicans to pass over their strongest candidate and nominate instead a candidate who will be easy to beat. For example, in 1948 the Democrats cooperated with the kingmakers to persuade Republicans to nominate a "me too" losing candidate, Tom Dewey, instead of the Republican Majority Leader, Bob Taft. The Democrats said they "hoped Republicans would nominate Taft" with the same reverse psychology that Brer Rabbit pleaded with the fox, "Oh, please don't throw me into the briar patch!"

After the 1948 election, the Democrats bragged about the trick they had pulled. Jack Redding, former publicity director of the Democratic National Committee, in his book INSIDE THE DEMOCRATIC PARTY, quoted Democratic National Chairman Robert Hannegan as saying in a Democratic strategy huddle:

> "If the Republicans were smart, they'd run Taft. He'd make a better candidate and would probably be harder for us to beat because he would fight harder. Don't make the mistake of underestimating Taft. The fact is Taft is a fighter and will make a terrific fight for what he represents. Dewey will be 'me too' all over again . . . Hit Taft hard and often; maybe we can stop him from getting the nomination and at the same time embarrass Dewey."

Harold Ickes put it more bluntly. He said:

"With the bases loaded, the Republicans
sent to the plate their bat boy. They could
have sent in their Babe Ruth—Bob Taft."

The question for Republicans at their 1964
National Convention was: At this crucial point
in American history, will we send in our bat
boy? Or will we send in our Babe Ruth — a
man who is not afraid or forbidden to take a
good cut at all major issues of the day?

America is best served when the two great
political parties compete with one another to the
fullest possible extent consistent with ethical con-
duct. It was in the forum of vigorous political
debate that the United States Constitution was
hammered out by the Founding Fathers. Abraham Lincoln rose to greatness from the platform
of hard-hitting partisan debates with Stephen A.
Douglas over issues that were just as important
to our country's survival as any issues today.

The secret of Anglo-American justice is the
competitive, adversarial trial system. Truth is
best served and favoritism eliminated by a procedure which requires the litigants to compete to
their maximum ability. There would be no justice
in our courts if opposing lawyers went through
an Alphonse and Gaston "me too" performance
and agreed with their opponents on key points.

Free competition has been the secret of America's greatness. Honest competition between our
producers, our transporters, our merchants, has
made the American economic system the envy of
the world. With only one-fifteenth of the world's

population, we produce over one-half of the world's goods. As sponsor of the great Sherman Anti-Trust Law, the Republican Party is especially dedicated to preserving and fostering competition.

Like trials, political campaigns should be competitive and adversarial. The Republican Party has a historic duty to demand that the major parties compete on foreign policy issues. Failure to compete in this field means a coverup of past mistakes. Free debate in this field will help us to avoid the same mistakes in the future and enable American voters to make the right choice on the basis of all the facts.

Chapter Four

The Smoke-Filled Room

1936

In early 1936 a little group of secret king-makers laid long-range plans to control the Republican Party. Their confidential meeting was in keeping with the political legend of the smoke-filled hotel room.

The presiding genius of this secret gathering in a royal suite on the 21st floor of the Waldorf-Astoria Hotel in New York was Thomas Lamont, senior partner in J. P. Morgan and Company, well-known international banking concern. Lamont was flanked to the right and left by Thomas Cochran, also of the Morgan firm, and by Alfred P. Sloan of General Motors. Five other prominent financiers and industrialists were also present.

The purpose of this august gathering was to consider possible Republican candidates for President against Franklin D. Roosevelt, who was then nearing the end of his first term.

We know from an account of this meeting by Dr. Glenn Frank,[1] President of the University of Wisconsin, who was present that the men in this select group spoke with the assurance that they would "decide" who the Republican nominee for President would be. The midwest was clamoring for recognition, and the eastern elite had decided that they would support a candidate from the corn belt.

Before the night was out, it was pretty well agreed that their support would be thrown to Governor Alf Landon of Kansas, who, of course, never stood a chance to win, because there was no beating Roosevelt for reelection in 1936.

One of the kingmakers at this secret meeting summed up the purpose of the meeting in these words:

"In the event we are not successful this year, *we* will select the candidate for 1940, and he will come from the East."

Support for Landon by the Lamont clique was sop for the midwest in a hopeless Republican year. The real goal was 1940 when, with the midwest presumably satisfied, the East would claim the right to name the nominee.

The choice of Landon was a significant one. The kingmakers such as "Ogden Mills, Eugene Meyer, Winthrop Aldrich recognized that . . . Landon might be adapted to their own purposes."[2] Landon had boasted, "I have cooperated with the New Deal to the best of my ability," and had even issued public praise of New Deal radical Rexford G. Tugwell.[3] It was not mere coincidence that the kingmakers passed over Herbert Hoover as too conservative, and vetoed Colonel Frank Knox for first place on the ticket because, although a liberal, he had attacked Marxism and Socialism in the New Deal.

When Landon was buried under an avalanche of electoral votes in 1936, the New York kingmakers breathed a collective sigh of relief that the Republican Party had escaped passing into control of the midwest.

Chapter Five

The Advertising Agent's Holiday

1940

As the 1940 election approached, the secret kingmakers met again in a hotel room in the Waldorf-Astoria in New York to decide who would be the Republican presidential candidate that year. They wanted someone who would be their willing tool, and whom they could rely on not to change or challenge the Roosevelt foreign policy. If their eastern candidate could have the "image" of a midwesterner, this would help to sell him to Republicans.

Suddenly someone suggested a New York lawyer named Wendell Willkie.

The kingmakers paused to think about the possibility of Wendell Willkie. He was a registered Democrat. Only five years before, he had been elected by Tammany Hall to the New York County Democratic Committee!¹ As a student at Indiana University, he had been a member of the Socialist Club.² He had never done anything in his entire life for the Republican Party. He was completely unknown outside his own limited circles. He was the high-salaried head of a large utility company. He had risen in the world as a lawyer who had successfully defended a large public utilities corporation against hundreds of personal-injury damage suits.

With all these handicaps, it was unthinkable that such a man, with such a background, could receive the highest honor the Republican Party confers. Unthinkable, that is, unless you know the power of the secret kingmakers and the "hidden persuaders" they are able to wield through their financial and propaganda contacts.

In spite of all his liabilities, the kingmakers decided Willkie was their man. They went to work to sell Willkie to the American public by a gigantic publicity spree. The columnist George Sokolsky called it "the advertising agent's holiday." Through their financial and other contacts throughout our communications media, they made it appear there was spontaneous public interest in Wendell Willkie.

Willkie was catapulted into the political arena by an article in the SATURDAY EVENING POST. The big buildup gained momentum as articles suggesting Willkie for the Republican nomination suddenly began to appear in leading newspapers and magazines. His picture spontaneously appeared on the covers of TIME and other popular magazines. He was given prestige in business circles by a favorable article in FORTUNE, and in popular circles by a feature article in LIFE. This unknown lawyer mysteriously appeared as an author in Sunday magazines.

There was no television in 1940, but there was radio, and the most popular program was "Information Please," then at the peak of its

Hooper rating and boasting 12 million listeners. It was arranged for Wendell Willkie to be a guest on "Information Please," where he surprised everyone by having his hand up more often and answering more questions than all the experts, even John Kieran. This radio program was loaded with technical questions about the United States Constitution, which were tailored for Willkie, the only lawyer on the panel.

On the chance that this program might be successful, the kingmakers were farsighted enough to have many pictures and a movie short made of it. After editing, the movie was shown in neighborhood movies all over the United States, and LIFE Magazine of April 22 featured a full page of pictures showing Willkie outsmarting all the intellectuals.

The Willkie boom was engineered by top advertising executives from Madison Avenue public relations firms such as Young and Rubicam, J. Walter Thompson, and Selvage and Smith.[3] Working individually and collectively, these publicity men planted news articles in magazines and newspapers, stimulated petitions, chain letters, advertisements, telegrams and fund-raising, and started Willkie Clubs and Willkie Mailing Committees. The advertising manager of Johns-Mansville organized the Indiana Box Supper to promote the legend of Willkie's rural background.

Seven weeks before the Republican Convention, the Gallup Poll reported that Willkie was the favorite of only three per cent of Republican

voters. Like the new cold remedies on the market
each winter, advertising turned Willkie into a
60-day wonder.

In 1940 the two leading contenders for the
Republican nomination were Thomas E. Dewey
and Senator Robert A. Taft. The New York
kingmakers considered Dewey an unacceptable
candidate because, in those days, Dewey was an
isolationist who stressed his Michigan birth and
education.

Governor Harold Stassen of Minnesota had
declared himself for Dewey and had invited
Dewey into the Minnesota primary and even
helped Dewey finance his campaign there. The
kingmakers looked upon the Minnesota situation
as a significant obstacle to Willkie because a defeat there could be dangerous to Willkie's mid-
western image.

The kingmakers are very resourceful, and it
didn't take them long to solve this problem.
Thomas Lamont discovered he had a relative
named John Cowles, who was publisher of the
Minneapolis STAR, a large newspaper strate-
gically important to Stassen's future. After a few
telephone calls, it was suggested to Stassen that
he go to New York and confer with some very
important people.

A delectable plum was dangled in front of the
ambitious Stassen: he was told he had been
selected to be Temporary Chairman of the Republican National Convention, in which capacity
he would deliver the Keynote Speech. In a few

days Stassen returned to Minnesota — no longer supporting Tom Dewey.

In order to receive the appointment as Temporary Chairman and Keynoter of the Convention, Stassen had to give a pledge to the Republican National Committee that he would remain neutral between all candidates for the nomination. Somehow this promise was forgotten; Stassen was so unneutral that he even served as Willkie's Floor Manager during the Convention. This was the first of many chores that Stassen has performed for the secret kingmakers.

As Convention time approached, one big stumbling block remained for Wendell Willkie — Senator Robert A. Taft. Knowledgeable observers could see that the race had narrowed itself to Willkie and Taft. Thinking that perhaps they might not be able to put Willkie over after all, and always wanting to have an alternate candidate waiting in the wings, the kingmakers decided to make a try at buying Taft.

The week before the Convention opened, Senator and Mrs. Taft were invited to a dinner party in New York given by Mr. and Mrs. Ogden Reid, publisher of the NEW YORK HERALD TRIBUNE. The details of the dinner party are set forth in ONE MAN: WENDELL WILLKIE by C. Nelson Sparks. The major facts have been thoroughly corroborated by both Robert Taft and Wendell Willkie.

The guest list for the Ogden Reid dinner party was carefully chosen. Present at this momentous

dinner party were Mr. Thomas Lamont, senior
partner of J. P. Morgan Company, and Mrs.
Lamont; Lord Lothian, then Ambassador to the
United States from Great Britain; Mr. and Mrs.
John Pillsbury of the Minneapolis milling family;
and Mr. and Mrs. Wendell Willkie. It was an
elegant dinner party, featuring the choicest duck
served in the highest style, with a liveried lackey
to wait on each guest.

Over cigars and coffee, the small talk was suddenly interrupted when the hostess announced
that those present would be favored with a few
remarks from Lord Lothian. The substance of
his little speech was that it was the duty of the
United States to go all out at once to aid Britain
in the war. This was in June of 1940, a year and
a half before Pearl Harbor. Thomas Lamont
was then called on, and he expressed himself as
fully in accord with Lord Lothian. Willkie was
called on next. He enthusiastically endorsed
everything that Lord Lothian and Lamont had
said. Willkie went all out for war, maintaining
that it was our duty to go to war at once to aid
England.

By this time, the plot was pretty clear to Taft.
He realized that he had been invited to the Reid
dinner for the purpose of ascertaining whether
he were willing to pay the price to get the support of the secret kingmakers for the Republican
nomination, namely, an all-out war declaration
that would satisfy the New York banking interests and the British Ambassador. Taft knew that

if he endorsed the remarks of Lothian, Lamont and Willkie, he would make himself acceptable to the powerful financial interests and thereby greatly improve his chance of winning the nomination.

Taft was a man of principle and he declined this rare opportunity to win the support of the kingmakers. When called on, he simply observed that he could add nothing to his remarks in the Senate, where he declared that Americans did not want to go to war to beat a totalitarian system in Europe if they were to get Socialism here when it is all over. Then Senator and Mrs. Taft left the party as soon as they could gracefully do so. A few days later, THE NEW YORK HERALD TRIBUNE announced its unequivocal support for Wendell Willkie with a three-column appeal to the delegates on the front page calling Willkie "Heaven's gift to the nation in its time of crisis."

When the Republican National Convention opened in Philadelphia, Willkie only had 105 Delegates. Even the Gallup Poll reported that Willkie was the favorite of only 17% of Republicans. Only the politically naive could believe that hundreds of Delegates suddenly went overboard for Willkie out of sheer fascination with the gravel voice and personality of "the barefoot boy from Wall Street."

A few Republicans saw through the publicity blitz at the time. Forty Republican Congressmen called for a "real Republican." Congressman

Usher Burdick declared:

> "I believe I am serving the best interests
> of the Republican Party by protesting in
> advance and exposing the machinations and
> attempts of J. P. Morgan and the other
> New York utility bankers in forcing Wen-
> dell Willkie on the Republican Party . . .
> There is nothing to the Willkie boom for
> President except the artificial public opinion
> being created by newspapers, magazines,
> and the radio. The reason back of all this
> is money. Money is being spent by someone
> and lots of it. This is a good time to find
> out whether the American people are to be
> let alone in the selection of a Republican
> candidate for the Presidency, or whether
> the 'special interests' of this country are
> powerful enough to dictate to the American
> people."[4]

Willkie had the support of the New York
kingmakers whose long fingers of money and
propaganda reached into every state. Their propaganda buildup for Willkie began to pay off
in Philadelphia where Thomas Lamont set up
headquarters. In addition, the kingmakers opened their bag of tricks for use at the Convention
itself. The "hidden persuaders" really went into
action.

The "get on the bandwagon" psychology was
played to the nth degree. The galleries were
packed with noisy Willkie supporters admitted
on forged tickets who chanted "we want Willkie"
to stampede the Convention. This chant was
used with the same repetition technique that ad-

vertisers developed for cigarettes.

Five dollar bills were given to taxi drivers to talk up Willkie. When Delegates would grab a cab to the Convention hall and ask the driver the obvious question, "How do things look?" the driver would reply, "It looks like everything is going to Willkie."

"Operation Telegram" was the most successful gimmick of the Willkie blitz. Nearly a million wires poured into Philadelphia for Willkie between Saturday and Tuesday.[5] In many of the larger cities all over the United States a few days before the Convention opened, pleasant female voices were calling prominent citizens and saying, "This is Western Union calling. Would you let us send the following telegram to your Delegates at the Convention in Philadelphia in behalf of Wendell Willkie?" The people called were prominent or important financially, but not politically wise. They were flattered at the thought of mixing in a small way with stirring political events. They did not realize they were paying for the telegrams; but they found them later on their phone bills.

Another phase of "Operation Telegram" was to shower a Delegate with wires from his clients or customers back home. For example, one Delegate was a successful automobile dealer who had gone to the Convention pledged to vote for another candidate. He received a telegram advocating Willkie's nomination from almost every man or woman to whom he had sold a Packard automobile. Many telegrams were not sent by the persons whose names were signed to them, and wires from all over the country showed unusual similarity in wording and misspellings. After the Delegate returned home and inquired, it was too late.

The kingmakers sought to influence Delegates by having the mortgage holders and bankers to whom they owed money call them in behalf of Willkie.[6] For example, one Delegate was called long distance by a miller in his home town who had annually advanced him money and seed on his season's crops. The miller, a Democrat, demanded that the Delegate vote for Willkie. Later the same day, the Delegate's banker who held the mortgage on his farm, called with the same demand. The Delegate voted for Willkie because he felt he had to.

The Willkie campaign was richly-financed, and money was spent freely before and during the Convention. The chairman of one delegation stated that he was offered $19,000 for the expenses of his delegation if he would deliver his state's vote for Willkie.[7] Another state was told to name its own price as payment for announcing a switch to Willkie. Powerful economic interests brought pressures on state delegations to force officeholders in line if they wanted to keep their jobs.

And so, the blitz was a success. The Republican Party, in Convention assembled, nominated Wendell Willkie for the presidency, with Taft a close second and Dewey farther behind. Willkie had no grassroots appeal and he ran a poor race, trailing the rest of the Republican ticket in most states. He failed to carry eleven states which at the same time elected Republican governors. His showing was pitiful in spite of the fact that he had the support of a long procession of prominent Democrats including two former Democratic presidential nominees, John W. Davis and Alfred E. Smith; former FDR braintrusters General Hugh Johnson and Raymond Moley; and many Democratic Governors and Senators. In no election since the Civil War had so many party leaders deserted their own party for the opposition. Many other senior Democrats were hostile to Roosevelt, but silent to preserve their party membership, including James A. Farley and Vice President John Garner.

After the election, Willkie was exposed as a complete phony. He cynically admitted under oath to a Senate committee that pledges he had made before the election were just "campaign oratory."[8] He hired an identified Soviet agent to ghost-write his book ONE WORLD. He eagerly donated his legal services to defend a top Communist named Schneiderman and take his case to the United States Supreme Court.

Those who might think Willkie's defeat bothered the New York kingmakers who had blitzed his nomination, just don't understand politics. The kingmakers did not care whether Willkie won or lost. All they cared was to make sure that they had on both tickets an eastern interventionist candidate who would continue Roosevelt's foreign policy so that the voters would not have a choice on the great issue of entering the European War. Their objective was to make sure that, if by chance a Republican should win, he would be a man the secret kingmakers could control. Their attitude was like that of the old time Philadelphia political boss who, when told his candidate could not win and would wreck the party, replied: "Yes, but we will own the wreckage."

Chapter Six
The Pollsters and the Hoaxers
1944

The New York kingmakers realized they could not capture the 1944 Republican nomination either with Willkie or with the same type of last-minute blitz they had used in 1940. This time they went into action earlier. They discovered and developed a new political weapon: the Gallup Poll. Dr. George Gallup began asking a lot of questions of a very few people, and — funny thing — he usually came up with answers that pleased the New York kingmakers.

The Gallup Poll has been used repeatedly as a subtle propaganda machine to sell the Republicans on the false propositions that the GOP cannot win unless it (1) continues the New Deal foreign policy and (2) names candidates who will appeal to left-leaning Democrats and liberals.

The Gallup Poll worked so well that, in 1944, there was hardly any need to have a Republican Convention. The Gallup Poll had already announced that Dewey had 68 percent of Republican voters in his camp, and that he was the only Republican with a chance to win. The Convention was cold, dull and colorless. The Delegates met merely to ratify the Gallup Poll decision.

Why did the kingmakers support Dewey in 1944 when they had fought him in 1940? Very simple. Dewey observed what happened in 1940 and how one gets to be the Republican nominee. Dewey decided to pay the price that Senator Taft had refused to pay at the Ogden Reid dinner. Dewey abandoned his isolationist views, joined with the New York internationalists, and himself became one of the powerful kingmakers.

It may be that, with World War II in full swing, no Republican could have been elected that year. Nevertheless, Dewey made a weak campaign and refused to mention, because of the personal request of George Marshall,[1] the best issue the Republicans had: how Roosevelt had invited and encouraged the Pearl Harbor attack. Dewey knew that Roosevelt had refused to negotiate with the pro-American government of Prince Konoye of Japan, and had given its successor an ultimatum which meant war. Dewey knew that we had broken the top Japanese code before Pearl Harbor. He knew that President Roosevelt, his Secretaries of War and Navy, and his Chief of Staff George Marshall, had advance warnings of the Japanese attack. He knew that Pearl Harbor was a disaster for which the Commander-in-Chief should be held personally responsible. Yet, he said nothing — and the voters failed to learn the truth.

After the votes were counted, the Roosevelt foreign policy was safe again from any effective challenge for four years. Roosevelt traveled to Yalta where he sold out our allies in Eastern Europe and China, and gave Stalin three votes in the United Nations.

Chapter Seven
Snatching Defeat from the Jaws of Victory

1948

The 1948 Republican nomination was a coveted prize. Two years earlier, the slogan "Had Enough?" and public reaction to price controls had given the Republican Party its largest victory of our time. On the principle that "coming events cast their shadows before them," Republicans confidently anticipated a sure win.

There was much resentment among conservative Republicans against the "me too" campaign Dewey had waged in 1944. There was a strong Republican Party tradition against nominating a loser, on the principle best expressed by Theodore Roosevelt's daughter, Alice Longworth, that "you can't make a souffle rise twice." But the Gallup Poll again hoaxed Republicans into nominating the choice of the New York kingmakers, Thomas E. Dewey.

To secure the nomination, the Dewey forces spent money and made deals and promises that Taft would never make. Offers were made of Federal jobs that Delegates could not resist. Mississippi's delegation was headed by a Taft man, but his Delegates voted the other way. After the vote, one Delegate ran for a train and died of a heart attack on it. He had $1,500 in fresh money on him and the other Delegates claimed it should be divided among them.[1]

One of the deals made by the Dewey managers was with Congressman Charles Halleck, who was promised the Vice Presidential nomination if he could deliver the Indiana delegation to Dewey. It wasn't easy, but Halleck delivered, confident that he would have second place on the ticket.

In the hours after Dewey was nominated President, the New York kingmakers, determined to continue the Roosevelt foreign policy, stepped in to scotch the deal. Speaking through their house organ, THE NEW YORK TIMES, the kingmakers declared:

> "Surely not Mr. Halleck! Mr. Halleck would bring into the campaign the perfect record of a Republican isolationist. Mr. Halleck voted against Selective Service in the summer of 1940 . . . Mr. Halleck voted against Lend-Lease . . . He voted against the British loan. He voted against the Hull reciprocal trade program in 1940 . . . With Mr. Taber he led the fight to cut appropriations under the Marshall Plan . . ."

Here was a good summary of what kind of a candidate the New York kingmakers will not tolerate. They will not permit a candidate on the ticket — even in second place — unless he has a foreign policy acceptable to the New York financiers and banking interests who profit so greatly from the New Deal foreign policy.

Dewey and the kingmakers chose Earl Warren of California as the Vice Presidential nominee. Before starting out on the campaign trail, Dewey and Warren promised each other that neither would mention the hottest issue of the day — the one on which the Democrats were most vulnerable — the issue of Communist infiltration in the Federal Government.

Even with the benefit of 20/20 hindsight, it is hard to see how Dewey could have lost. The Democrats were hopelessly split, with the Southerners supporting Strom Thurmond and the left-wing radicals supporting Henry Wallace.

Truman pitched his campaign against the Republican 80th Congress. Dewey made a fatal mistake when he did not defend it. The Republican 80th Congress, under the leadership of Senator Robert Taft, had made the greatest record of any Congress in the 20th century. For the first time since the start of the New Deal, it reduced taxes, balanced the budget, and reduced the national debt. It exposed Alger Hiss, Harry Dexter White and other Communists in the New Deal. It launched the Greek-Turkish Military Aid Plan which under General Van Fleet crushed the Communist guerillas in Greece. It enacted the Taft-Hartley Law over Truman's veto. It rejected Truman's plan to draft railroad strikers into the Army. It authorized the Hoover Commission to reorganize the Government. It passed the 22nd Amendment to the Constitution limiting the President to two terms. By any standard, it was a constructive, responsible Congress, and would have been a winning issue for Republicans.

By his incredible "me too" campaign, by his refusal to debate the issues of the 80th Congress and Communism in Government, Dewey truly snatched defeat from the jaws of victory.[2] Republicans found to their sorrow that Dewey could not Gallup into the White House as he had Galluped into the nomination.

But again, Dewey's defeat did not bother the kingmakers at all. All they wanted was to make sure there was a candidate on both tickets who would rubberstamp their America Last foreign policy.

The 1948 election results should have destroyed the Gallup Poll as a weapon which could again capture the presidential nomination. Gallup predicted that Dewey would be elected in a landslide. Leading liberal opinion-makers such as Walter Lippmann were so carried away by misplaced confidence in Gallup that they suggested we dispense with the election, save that national expense, and simply declare Dewey the winner over Truman.

It is time the American people wake up to the inaccuracy of the Gallup Poll. In ancient times, superstitious people used to go to the temple and beg a prophecy from some priestess who belonged to an elite cult. The batting average of these ancient frauds was at least as good as the Gallup Poll. The famous Delphic Oracle built up a phony reputation as a prophet by giving trick answers subject to contradictory interpretations. To the question: Who will win the war between Athens and Sparta, the Oracle answered: "I say to you Sparta, the Athenians will conquer."

Likewise, the Gallup Poll has built its reputation by asking trick questions. Ask a loaded question and get a loaded answer.

Author and political analyst Svend Petersen made a thorough statistical analysis of the presidential polls taken by George Gallup and compared them with the presidential polls taken by the old LITERARY DIGEST which went out of existence after predicting that Landon would defeat Roosevelt in 1936. His conclusion: the LITERARY DIGEST scored three victories and one failure; the Gallup Poll achieved one victory, one failure, and in two elections Gallup reported such a large percentage of voters "who had not made up their minds" that his poll could not be called either a success or failure.[3]

It is too bad for American politics that the Gallup Poll did not have the good grace (like the LITERARY DIGEST) after its abysmal failure in 1948, to fold its tent and silently steal away.

It should be noted that the LITERARY DIGEST polled millions, while George Gallup polls only a few hundred — so few that the exact number is a dark secret which Gallup will not reveal. Were he to reveal the pathetic paucity of his pollees, the myth of the Gallup Poll would join the myth of the Delphic Oracle in the limbo of history.

Chapter Eight

The Big Steal

1952

For long in advance, it was easy for everyone to see that 1952 would be a crucial election year, and a good year for Republicans. The Truman scandals, the Korean War, Communist infiltration in Government, the fact that for the first time since 1932 the GOP was not faced with an incumbent President — all these factors combined to make the Republican nomination an even greater prize than in 1948.

The obvious choice was Senator Robert A. Taft, the man who was the acknowledged leader of the Republican Party in good years as well as bad, who had one of the most honorable and distinguished records of Government service of any man alive, who was respected by both friends and enemies, who was the choice of the overwhelming majority of organization Republicans.

The kingmakers vetoed Taft. It has been said that "Hell hath no fury like a woman scorned." What the American public was to learn in 1952 was that "Hell hath no fury like the New York kingmakers scorned." Taft had scorned them at the Ogden Reid dinner party in 1940. The kingmakers knew he was not one of them. They could not control him. He was dedicated to reduce the level of Federal spending. Most important, he would never condone the America Last policy of the New Deal. Taft's own book A FOREIGN POLICY FOR AMERICA was based on this simple premise (which was anathema to the kingmakers):

> "The ultimate purpose of our foreign policy must be to protect the liberty of the people of the United States."

The kingmakers' propagandists launched a potent word missile: "I like Taft, but Taft can't win." This slogan was cleverly designed to drive a wedge between Taft and his supporters, and it probably did affect many people. Of course it was completely false, as Taft had the best vote-getting record of any Republican in the country, and had proved this ability in Ohio in his tremendous 1950 victory, in spite of dire predictions to the contrary. During the preferential primaries held in 1952, Taft polled more popular votes than any other Republican candidate.

The kingmakers selected their 1952 candidate carefully — General Dwight Eisenhower. It should be made perfectly clear that nothing in these pages is meant to cast any reflection whatsoever on Eisenhower. He was an amateur in politics; he did not have the slightest idea of the tactics used by the little clique determined to steal the nomination and push him into the Presidency.

Eisenhower was a long-time favorite of the kingmakers. Several years before, they had plac-

ed him in an important non-political job to keep
him in the public eye, but not require him to take
a stand on controversial questions such as the
Taft-Hartley Act and Communists in our Government. They had installed him as President of
Columbia University. With all due respect to
Ike's many talents, he was not suited for this
position. Yet, the kingmakers found Ike's lack of
qualifications no handicap because some of the
kingmakers were trustees of Columbia University.

In order to make sure they retained control
of the 96-vote delegation at the 1952 Republican
National Convention, the kingmakers persuaded
Thomas E. Dewey to run for a third term as
Governor of New York in 1950. By orders of
Winthrop Aldrich of the Chase National (Rockefeller) Bank, Lieutenant Governor Joe R. Hanley, who was to have been the candidate, was
bludgeoned into withdrawing. Hanley revealed
in a letter which leaked out that he had been
"humiliated" and was "disappointed and heart-
sick" over the pressure put on him, but he had
withdrawn on the promise that his debts would be
paid and he would be given a fat state job.

The secret kingmakers never put all their eggs
in one basket. They always have a stand-in waiting in the wings. Just on the outside chance that
they might not be able to sell Ike to the Republican Party, they had placed their second choice,
Harold Stassen, on ice as President of the University of Pennsylvania. Stassen was even less

qualified to be a University president than Eisenhower.

The New York kingmakers reactivated the whole propaganda apparatus that they had created to publicize Wendell Willkie. The Madison Avenue public relations firms, the big national magazines, and four-fifths of the influential newspapers in the country turned themselves into propaganda organs to build the Eisenhower image. For months and months, Ike's picture was on the cover of magazines and we were inundated with articles proposing him for the Republican nomination.

But even all this fantastic propaganda buildup, arranged through the diverse financial contacts of the New York kingmakers, could not have won the nomination for Eisenhower had it not been for the vicious and dishonest "hidden persuaders" used just prior and during the Convention itself. Of course thousands of sincere people were genuinely for Eisenhower; just as thousands of sincere people were for General Douglas MacArthur. The point is that Eisenhower could not have been successful without the vicious tactics used by the New York kingmakers determined to destroy Taft.

These tactics started early in 1952 in the New Hampshire primary, although we didn't learn about these "hidden persuaders" until long after. Ike-supporter Tex McCrary himself admitted that he had used dirty tactics against Taft in that crucial primary. He said:

> "I planted people in every Taft audience.
> I would have mothers get up to say, 'I have
> a son who is being drafted — and he wants
> to ask you why your voting record is the
> same as Marcantonio's'."

Of course this was a loaded question, as Taft's
voting record was the opposite of pro-Communist
Marcantonio. But such tactics had their effect,
and New Hampshire was Taft's first setback.[1]

Taft was beset by repeated attacks that had
no regard for truth and decency. Arthur Hays
Sulzberger, publisher of the NEW YORK
TIMES, said that his newspaper was opposing
Taft's presidential nomination "because it is so
frightened at the thought of Mr. Taft."[2]

As time for the Republican Convention approached, it became apparent that Taft had
enough Delegates to win the nomination on the
first ballot. Eisenhower was at least 150 Delegates short. The New York kingmakers were
desperate. They had to come up with some trick,
some gimmick, some "hidden persuader", to capture a crucial few Delegates from Taft.

The opportunity presented itself in Texas.
They devised a scheme whereby they would ig-
nore the legally-elected Taft Delegates. hold
rump meetings to which they would invite Democrats who had no intention of voting for any
Republican in the November election, and have
this illegal body "elect" Eisenhower Delegates,
who would then try to unseat the Taft Delegates
at the Convention.

The Eisenhower managers ran advertisements in Texas newspapers, and mailed vast quantities of postcards addressed to "Occupant", which invited Democrats to come to Republican Party meetings and "vote" for Eisenhower. These ads stated: "You are not pledged to support the nominee of the Republican Party nor does it prohibit you from voting in the July Democratic Primary nor does it prohibit you from voting for whomever you please in the November election."

These advertisements fraudulently represented that Democrats — who intended to remain Democrats — could elect Delegates to the Republican National Convention. Such a procedure was clearly contrary to Texas law. The advertisements and postcards urged voters to do what Texas law expressly prohibits.

(One of the reasons why this is wrong was aptly stated by one Republican: "If this procedure were allowed, all Republicans would need to do to win would be to send their members into Democratic primaries and party conventions and nominate Alger Hiss!")

When Taft and his supporters protested this illegal action, one of the kingmakers' hatchet men came up with a brainstorm — accuse Taft of stealing Delegates!

The first newspaper to shout "the big steal" was the HOUSTON POST, whose owner, Oveta Culp Hobby, was later rewarded by appointment as Secretary of Health, Education and Welfare. Suddenly, as though someone had pressed a button, the whole propaganda apparatus of our country went into action to slander the character of the most honorable man in public life. Our whole communications media echoed with the slogan "Thou shalt not steal." The "big steal" issue was expanded to take in Georgia and Louisiana, too. TIME Magazine came out with a special edition on Monday of Convention week so that every Delegate could be provided with the issue accusing Taft of the "big steal". Masked bandits with guns paraded the streets of Chicago carrying placards which read "Taft steals votes", and oversize signs appeared proclaiming RAT stands for Robert A. Taft.

How the liberal press picked up and spread the smear against Taft can be best described in the words of Allen Drury in ADVISE AND CONSENT:

> "All the vast publicity machine that always goes into concerted action for a liberal cause had gone to work . . .; an operation so honed and smoothed and refined over the years that none of its proprietors even had to consult with one another. The instinct had been alerted, the bell had rung, the national salivations had come forth on schedule."

Eisenhower had no real knowledge of the tactics used by his supporters to steal the nomination. When he learned of what was happening in Texas, he stated at a press conference: "I myself would never have put in such advertisement in such a paper."[3] This, in effect, constituted a repudiation of all the claims of "dishonesty" and "fraud" made by Henry Cabot Lodge, Sherman Adams and the Eisenhower managers. This, in effect, was an admission by Eisenhower that it was his own supporters who were guilty of fraud in Texas.

When the illegally-elected Eisenhower Delegates arrived at the Republican National Convention in Chicago, the job was to get them officially seated in place of the Taft Delegates, in order to take away Taft's narrow margin of victory. By high-pressure propaganda and hypocritical bleating about the moral issue, the kingmakers brought about a change in the rules under which every previous Convention had functioned. Although this rules change was contrary to common sense as well as every principle of parliamentary procedure, it was called the "fair play amendment."

After the rules were changed, the second battle at the 1952 Convention was over the seating of the contested Delegates. By promising Earl Warren the first appointment to the Supreme Court and Richard Nixon the Vice Presidency, the kingmakers persuaded the California delegation — without hearing any of the evidence — to vote to expel the Georgia, Louisiana and Texas Delegates and seat the Eisenhower Delegates.

The California delegation, as well as the New York and other crucial delegations, were told to vote for the Eisenhower Delegates in the contests, regardless of the merits of the case, regard-

less of the evidence, regardless of the judicial
determinations of party conventions in the states
and supporting court decisions, regardless of the
hours of open hearings in the Republican Party's
own tribunals, the National Committee and the
Credentials Committee. This was called "fair
play."

The pressure put on Delegates on the issue
of the contested Delegates was apparent to spec-
tators at the hearings held by the Credentials
Committee. The Pennsylvania representative on
this committee was a fair-minded judge who,
although in the Eisenhower camp, voted to award
the contested Delegates to Taft because he believed that was the just verdict after hearing the
evidence. The following day, he returned to the
hearing and reversed his vote. Pressure from
Governor John S. Fine had turned him into a
shaken and humiliated man, required to vote
against his conscience. Fine himself had been
brought into line by the kingmakers with the
promise that he could dispense all Federal pat-
ronage in Pennsylvania.[4]

Tom Dewey was there reminding his New
York delegation that he would remain governor
for another two and a half years, and that he
had "a long memory."[5] He reminded the Delegates of the control he had over state jobs. Any
Delegate who disobeyed Dewey had to be prepared to lose his job, or have his relative or friend
lost his job. Taft had pledges from 17 New York
Delegates but, after the Dewey ukase, only four

dared to vote for Taft on the contested Delegates, the same courageous four who had attended General Douglas MacArthur's Keynote Speech on the first night of the Convention, in defiance of Dewey's orders. None of the other 92 Dewey-controlled Delegates was permitted to attend the Keynote Speech of the Convention they were elected to participate in.

Sherman Adams was there, presumably making the same kind of deals with state delegations that he later made with Bernard Goldfine for a vicuna coat and a Turkish rug. Winthrop Aldrich, President of the Chase Manhattan Bank, was there; for his pre-Convention services he was appointed Ambassador to England. Henry Ford II was there, with his yacht in Lake Michigan equipped to entertain wavering Delegates, and to provide a fleet of Mercuries with drivers for the use of pro-Ike Delegates. Eisenhower managers whispered that Delegates who held out for Taft would be marked for life.

When the Convention opened, the Taft headquarters had the signed pledges of 604 Delegates, the narrow majority he needed out of 1,203. Eisenhower had only 400 plus. But the attrition of the "hidden persuaders" whittled away at Taft's majority and cost the margin of victory. The Taft headquarters received reports of Delegates who were bodily put on the train for home, leaving their alternates to vote for Ike. Delegates were threatened with loss of their jobs and calling of their bank loans, unless they voted for Eisenhower. Money flowed in great quantities everywhere.

One of the Chicago newspapers summed up the Convention like this:

> "While yelling, 'Steal!', they stole. While piously condemning evil, they entered the bagnio with it. With holy airs, they prejudged the issues, and with piety — and a hope of patronage — they cried corruption while corrupting their own small souls. It was a sickening spectacle.
>
> "On Monday the cry was 'fair play.' On Wednesday all pretense of fairness was forsaken. On Monday the old rules of 1948 were bad. On Wednesday the bad old rules and precedents of 1948 were cited by the same people, and now they were good. The rule of seating Delegates in 1948 was lamentable on Monday. On Wednesday the precedent of 1948 was invoked to seat Delegates, so long as they were for Eisenhower."[6]

So the Convention, by a small margin, without hearing any of the evidence, overruled the Credentials Committee, overruled the Republican National Committee, threw out the Taft Delegates from Georgia, Texas and Louisiana, and seated Eisenhower Delegates.

After the votes were counted on the issue of the contested Delegates, it was all over but the shouting. On the first ballot, Eisenhower received 595 votes — nine short of victory. Suddenly Harold Stassen's Minnesota banner waved frantically and swung to Ike the winning bloc of 16 votes.

In the fall of 1952, Senator Robert A. Taft prepared his own analysis of why he lost the Republican nomination the preceding July. He correctly and forcefully described the reasons as follows:

> "First, it was the power of the New York financial interest and a large number of businessmen subject to New York influence . . . Second, four-fifths of the influential newspapers in the country were opposed to me continuously and vociferously and many turned themselves into propaganda sheets for my opponent.
>
> "The making of a moral issue out of the Texas case was only possible because every internationalist paper sent special writers to blow up a contest which ordinarily would have been settled fairly by the National Committee and the Credentials Committee. . . . If there had not been these issues, the publicity firms would have invented others to be shouted by the pro-Eisenhower press."[7]

Eisenhower was not responsible for any of the vicious tactics used to win his nomination. Taft did not blame him, and no responsible Republican blames him. He repudiated the illegal tactics used by his managers in Texas.

After the nomination, the Eisenhower managers started to lead Eisenhower through the same empty campaign and meaningless oratory that had characterized Willkie and Dewey. Some forthright spokesmen in the Eisenhower camp began publicly to express their concern. The pro-

Ike Scripps-Howard newspapers cried out in an-
guish that Eisenhower's campaign was "running
like a dry creek."

As a result, General Eisenhower personally
seized control of his campaign and called on
Senator Taft for help. On September 12, 1952,
they met in New York and issued a campaign document which gave the voters a choice on foreign
policy, the first choice in 20 years. This document, called the Morningside Declaration said:

> "General Eisenhower will give this coun-
> try an administration inspired by Republi-
> can principles of continued and expanding
> liberty for all as against the continued
> growth of New Deal socialism which we
> would suffer under Governor Stevenson,
> representative of the left-wingers, if not a
> left-winger himself."

Speaking in Buffalo, New York, General Eisenhower promised to "clean out the State Department from top to bottom." He approved
the campaign slogan: "Corruption, Communism,
and Korea." General Eisenhower and all Republican candidates in 1952 campaigned on the Republican Party Platform adopted by the 1952
Convention which promised:

> "We shall eliminate from the State De-
> partment and from every Federal office,
> all, wherever they may be found, who
> share responsibility for the needless predi-
> caments and perils in which we find our-
> selves. We shall also sever from the public
> payroll the hoards of loafers, incompetents
> and unnecessary employees who clutter

the administration of our foreign affairs. . . . The Government of the United States, under Republican leadership, will repudiate all commitments contained in secret understandings such as those of Yalta which aid Communist enslavements. . . . We shall again make liberty into a beacon light of hope that will penetrate the dark places . . . We shall see to it that no treaty or agreement with other countries deprives our citizens of the rights guaranteed them by the Federal Constitution. . . . There are no Communists in the Republican Party . . . We never compromised with Communism and we have fought to expose it and to eliminate it in government and American life. A Republican President will appoint only persons of unquestioned loyalty. . . . Reduction of expenditures by the elimination of waste and extravagance so that the budget will be balanced and a general tax reduction can be made."

To the dismay of the kingmakers, as well as of the liberals and Democrats, the Republican Party closed ranks. Aided by Senator Joseph McCarthy's television analysis of candidate Stevenson's soft-on-Communism record, Republicans offered the people the choice they had been denied for four presidential elections. The result is history.

The kingmakers were somewhat nonplused at Eisenhower's victory and its meaning. His election in November was a clear mandate to repudiate the New Deal foreign policy, stop coddling

Communists, win the war in Korea, end corruption in Government, and cut Federal spending.

The kingmakers are very resourceful. They moved quietly and efficiently to guarantee that the Republican campaign pledges of 1952 would not be fulfilled. Their task was made easy because Eisenhower was, admittedly, an amateur in politics. He was as out of his depth as Taft would have been as Commander of SHAEF.

Eisenhower did his best and loyally stood by Ezra Taft Benson and Richard Nixon when the kingmakers tried to force them out of his official family. But after eight years, the objective observer has to admit that we still had the same America Last foreign policy, there was no housecleaning in the State Department, we accepted a stalemate instead of victory in Korea, and Federal spending was higher than ever.

Moreover, those eight years saw steady deterioration in the strength of the Republican Party. Eisenhower never could transfer his magnetism to other Republican candidates. Eisenhower could not elect a Republican Congress in 1954, 1956 or 1958 and could not elect his hand-picked successor, Richard Nixon, running against a little known Senator from a small state in 1960.

In 1951, before Eisenhower's election, there were 25 Republican Governors. In 1959 there were only 14. In 1951, there were 47 Republican Senators and 199 Republican Congressmen; in 1959 there were only 34 Senators and 153 Con-

gressmen. In 1951 there were 754 Republican
State Senators and 2566 Republican State Representatives, in 1959 there were only 592 and
1942 respectively. After seven years of President
Eisenhower's leadership, the Republicans had lost
24% of the vital offices they had held BEFORE
his election.

Taft was one of the first Republicans to wake
up to how the kingmakers, after using Eisenhower to win the election, promptly used him
as a cover for the perpetuation of the Roosevelt-
Truman foreign policy and the failure to fulfill
the Republican Platform of 1952. In the White
House on April 30, 1953, before a dozen Congressmen and others, Taft told President Eisenhower:

> "You're taking us right down the same
> road that Truman traveled. It's a repudia-
> tion of everything we promised in the
> (1952) campaign."

As the years passed, most of those who had
stolen the Republican nomination for Eisenhower
departed involuntarily from the political scene.
In the same election that Eisenhower won, Senator Henry Cabot Lodge was defeated for reelection by John F. Kennedy. Sherman Adams,
Ike's chief administrative assistant, had to beat
a hasty retreat from public life after revelations
that he had accepted a vicuna coat and a Turkish
rug for interceding for Bernard Goldfine. Oveta
Culp Hobby resigned as Secretary of Health,
Education and Welfare, after her Department

had to take responsibility for the costly pre-
mature licensing of the Salk polio vaccine. Herbert Brownell resigned as Attorney General after
legal scholars pointed out that he gave President
Eisenhower bad advice on Little Rock and should
have used marshals instead of Federal soldiers.[8]
Donald Eastvold, Attorney General of the State
of Washington, who was the star speaker for
the kingmakers on the issue of the contested
Delegates, warning the Delegates of the grave
moral turpitude they would commit if they seated
Taft's southern Delegates, abandoned his political career and left his own state. Paul Hoffman, one of those who had persuaded Eisenhower to enter politics, failed in his efforts to
keep the American Studebaker plants operating
and finally married a prominent liberal Democrat, Anna Rosenberg. Harold Stassen has since
sustained a steady succession of lopsided defeats in the primaries, proving that his kingmaker support was not shared by the voters.

Chapter Nine

Here Comes That Man Again

1956

As the Republican Convention of 1956 approached, the renomination of President Eisenhower was a foregone conclusion. There was a little flurry about Ike's heart attack, but the pros never considered the possibility of running any other candidate. Republicans looked forward to a joyful Convention in San Francisco.

The uncertainty about Eisenhower's physical condition, however, did give the kingmakers serious concern about the Vice Presidential nominee. The kingmakers had accepted Richard Nixon in 1952 because he had helped to deliver the California delegation to the Eisenhower faction on the first crucial issues.

But the kingmakers never really trusted Nixon for two reasons: (1) he was not a creature of their own making, therefore he was not beholden to them; and (2) he had risen to fame as an anti-Communist investigator, as one of those chiefly responsible for the prosecution of Alger Hiss. For this, the Democrats hated him with the unreasoning partisan reaction that caused Harry Truman to call the Hiss case " a red herring"; the Liberal Establishment would never forgive him; and the secret kingmakers were afraid of him because they consistently oppose raising either the domestic or foreign issue of Communism. They fear that it will open a Pandora's Box of public reaction which might bring about a change in the America Last pro-Communist foreign policy in which they have a vested interest.

With the reins of the Presidency held only by the strings of Ike's injured heart, the kingmakers decided to dump Nixon from the Republican ticket.

The kingmakers whistled, and again came forth their faithful friend and ally, Harold Stassen, who was at the time Special Assistant on Disarmament Problems, a position that gave him Cabinet status. At a formal news conference on July 23, 1956, Stassen announced his support of Governor Christian A. Herter of Massachusetts, calling him "6%" stronger than Nixon as a Vice-Presidential candidate. Stassen was granted a four-week leave of absence from the Eisenhower Administration to pursue his campaign to persuade the Republicans to drop Nixon.[1]

To the general public, this appeared to be a one-man crusade that spontaneously picked up momentum as Stassen issued each new statement. To the discerning observer, however, there was more to this tactic than met the eye. There was behind-the-scenes support in very high places. There was mysterious financial support. In the background were a number of powerful but shadowy figures. One of these was identified by the Chief of the UPI Washington bureau as General Lucius Clay.[2]

The key to this maneuver was the choice of Christian Herter. Why was he, of all Republicans, selected? Herter was a man with no particular talent or national following. He was a poor public speaker and, since he was badly crippled by arthritis, he was even less physically vigorous than Eisenhower after his heart attack.

Herter was picked because he was a reliable ally of the kingmakers and the foreign policy they sought to preserve. As a Congressman from Massachusetts, he had sponsored in the House of Representatives the foreign aid bill which became known as the Marshall Plan, which proved to be so financially profitable to the kingmakers. He had helped to organize the Council on Foreign Relations which has been the chief sponsor of the disastrous America Last foreign policy.

When the kingmakers discovered that Nixon was so strong with organization Republicans that they could not dump him without endangering Ike's own reelection, they gave up and Herter made the nominating speech for Nixon. When Herter completed his tedious speech at the Cow Palace, the Delegates breathed a sigh of relief that one so lacking in popular appeal was not their Vice Presidential candidate.

Christian A. Herter was rewarded for his part in the dump-Nixon move by being named Under Secretary of State. When John Foster Dulles died, Herter was advanced to Secretary of State, a post for which he had no known qualifications — except that he had been cleared by the kingmakers as a certified sponsor of huge foreign handouts.

Herter presided over the worst blunder in the 100-year history of the Republican Party. It was under Herter that the U.S. State Department, ignoring the reports from our Ambassadors to Cuba, assisted Castro to power.

Chapter Ten

Surrender in Manhattan

1960

Immediately after Eisenhower and Nixon were reelected in 1956, the secret kingmakers realized that Richard Nixon would be the front-runner at the 1960 Convention. They laid their plans early and carefully.

This time their candidate was Nelson Rockefeller, whose political career had been nourished at just the right speed as Governor of New York, and whose image had been carefully built by a full-fledged image-making organization with a staff of 70 persons comprising six divisions with separate functions.

Rockefeller jumped with both feet into the 1960 race, and ran hard. Rockefeller's campaign was noteworthy for the way he removed himself from the "mainstream" of Republican policy by opposing the Eisenhower-Nixon position and agreeing with the Democrat position on such key issues as the mythical "missile gap", the U-2 incident, and medicare.

A few weeks before the Republican Convention was to open in Chicago, the kingmakers surveyed the situation. They faced the hard reality that Nixon had carefully built his political fences within the Republican Party for many years, his organization support was solid, and he would be difficult if not impossible to defeat for the nomination.

The New York kingmakers are resourceful and persistent. They decided that, if they couldn't beat him, they would try to influence him. They fell back on the tactic they had tried with Senator Taft at the Ogden Reid dinner in June of 1940.

And so it came to pass that, on the Saturday before the Republican Convention opened in Chicago, Nixon made a pilgrimage to New York where he met for eight hours at Rockefeller's Fifth Avenue apartment. At the conclusion of that meeting, Nixon agreed to accept the changes in the Republican Platform that Rockefeller demanded.

The Republican Platform Committee had been meeting in Chicago for an entire week, laboriously pounding out the Platform which would reflect the views of Republicans from all the 50 states. Now the Platform Committee was handed the Rockefeller-Nixon orders: Throw out your week's work, the money and time you have spent at your own expense to come to Chicago and hear witnesses and draft a document to submit to the Convention, throw it all out and accept the Rockefeller-Nixon Platform worked out in secret 700 miles from the Convention.

Republicans everywhere understood the meaning and significance of the new Rockefeller-Nixon alliance. It meant much more than mere

changes of words in the Platform. It meant
that Nixon had paid the price that Taft had been
unwilling to pay. He had purged himself of his
independence and made himself acceptable to the
New York kingmakers. Rank and file Republicans knew that this forbode a turn toward the
same "liberal me-tooism" which had twice defeated Dewey.

Senator Barry Goldwater promptly labelled
the new Nixon alliance a "surrender to Rockefeller".[1] Goldwater said the entire Convention
had been the victim of an "unprecedented last-
minute attempt" to impose a platform dictated
by "a spokesman for the ultra-liberals." Goldwater interpreted Nixon's mission to New York
as "paying court on the leader of the Republican
left", and as "a bid to appease the Republican
left."

Goldwater continued with a statement that
was remarkable both for its candor and its pro-
phetic nature. He said: "I believe this to be immoral politics. I also believe it to be self-defeat-
ing." He predicted that the Rockefeller-Nixon
agreement will "live in history as the Munich of
the Republican Party" and will guarantee "a
Republican defeat in November."

As his part of the bargain, Rockefeller made a
seconding speech for Nixon at the Convention.
To the bewilderment of the television audience,
Rockefeller nominated "Richard E. (for Mil-
hous) Nixon". A Rockefeller intimate later explained this mistake: "Rocky imagined he was

nominating Thomas E. Dewey."

Nixon confirmed his new alliance by accepting as his running mate one of the darlings of the internationalist clique, one of the discredited hatchet men of the smear-Taft maneuver in 1952, and also of the get-McCarthy cabal of 1954, Henry Cabot Lodge.

Newspaper reporter Edward Lindsay summed up the surrender like this:

> "The Republican Party now stands not only left of the late Senator Robert A. Taft, but somewhat pointedly left of President Eisenhower."[2]

The result of Nixon's surrender was that, like Willkie and Dewey before him, Nixon pulled his punches and failed to campaign on the fundamental issues. He beat a steady retreat from the conservative and anti-Communist principles which alone could bring victory for Republicans. Nixon's surrender to Rockefeller was not productive; Rockefeller failed to carry his own state for Nixon.

Republicans should remember that the kingmakers are quite willing to have their candidate talk like a real Republican when seeking the nomination. But once he is nominated, then a Dr. Jekyll and Mr. Hyde transformation takes place, and he switches from a fiery fighter to a milktoast "me too" candidate. Kingmaker candidates are brainwashed into acting like they would rather be anti-right than be president.

Henry Cabot Lodge's campaign disappointed

even the liberals. According to NEWSWEEK, "His laziness became legend. The Lodge entourage started the day late and shut up shop early. He canceled an upstate New York visit to take his wife to Niagara Falls on the Canadian side." He canceled five of seven appearances in Kansas City in order to watch TV.[3]

After the 1960 election, it was not hindsight, but sorrow that his foresight had proved so accurate, when Senator Goldwater said the Nixon-Lodge ticket lost "not because we were Republicans but because we were not Republican enough." Goldwater analyzed what happened to rank-and-file Republicans during the 1960 campaign like this:

> "Eighty per cent of the delegates to the Republican National Convention in 1960 were Conservatives. They felt let down by the platform. . . . In the campaign, they became disenchanted; Nixon appeared to be just another me-too candidate . . . These people do not feel that their concept of Republicanism is being reflected at the leadership level."[4]

And the kingmakers? Did they shed any tears when Nixon and Lodge lost? Oh no; they were not unhappy at all. They never liked Nixon very much anyway, and Lodge always was considered expendable. The kingmakers breathed a sigh of relief, secure in the knowledge that Nixon was shelved, and the America Last foreign policy would continue under Kennedy and Johnson and their coterie of ADA advisers.

Chapter Eleven

The Obvious Choice

1964

By mid-1963, impartial observers could see that the Republican Party had one obvious, logical, deserving, winning candidate. He combined the integrity of Robert A. Taft with the glamour of Dwight Eisenhower. He had proved his ability to win against heavy odds. He was truly *a national* candidate with a demonstrated following in all the 50 states. For the first time, Republicans had a candidate with genuine appeal to the youth of America. When Senator Barry Goldwater at long last announced he would be a candidate, this was in response to a genuine grass-roots movement — not the result of a publicity blitz.

This obvious candidate had been a success at everything he has tried. Like Eisenhower, this obvious candidate is a General, and like Taft he has vast political experience. He is the epitome of American constitutional principles.

He was a successful businessman. He is a successful author; his two books were best-sellers: THE CONSCIENCE OF A CONSERVATIVE and WHY NOT VICTORY? He had a distinguished World War II record; he has risen to the rank of Major General in the Air Force

Reserve, and he still pilots jet fighter planes, a remarkable feat for one of his age and position.

He has been a tremendous success in politics. He was twice elected Senator from Arizona, a state where the Democratic registrations outnumber Republicans two to one. He successfully held one of the most important jobs in the Republican Party: Chairman of the Republican Senatorial Campaign Committee. He is the most sought-after speaker in the United States today.

The obvious nominee of the Republican Party in 1964 was Senator Barry Goldwater.

Goldwater has the magic quality of leadership that is based on independence of thought and courage. An almost-forgotten incident in his legislative career proves how the Goldwater brand of leadership can prevail even when a minority of one.

In 1959 the Senate passed what was popularly known as the Kennedy "sweetheart" labor bill by the staggering margin of 90 to 1. Senator Goldwater was the lone dissenter. He voted against the bill on the ground that it allowed Senator Kennedy, a presidential aspirant, to give the appearance of sponsoring labor reform legislation; whereas, his bill could be properly described as like a flea bite on the hide of a bull elephant. The entire press predicted that Senator Goldwater's dissent was a futile gesture and that the Kennedy bill would pass the House quickly and become law.

Then a remarkable thing happened. Because

of the brilliant way that Senator Goldwater had focused attention on the issue of monopoly versus freedom, our Congressmen began to hear from their constituents back home.

As a result, it was not the Kennedy "sweetheart" bill, but a real labor reform bill called the Landrum-Griffin Act, which passed the House and ultimately became law as a substitute for the Kennedy bill.

Senator Goldwater gave us dramatic proof that conservatism is popular. He showed that a minority of one can ultimately be victorious against overwhelming odds.

Any political leader can score a win if he has the votes in his pocket, just as any general can win if he has more men and more weapons. The true test of leadership is the ability to carry your side to victory when the odds are against you. This is the kind of leadership Barry Goldwater has demonstrated in a political way in Arizona, and in a legislative way in the Senate.

This is leadership that can win elections and solve problems at home, and defeat the Communists abroad. This is the leadership for which America yearns today.

Most important, Barry Goldwater is the one Republican who can and will win — because he will campaign on the issues of 1964. He is the one Republican who will not pull his punches to please the kingmakers. He can be counted on to face the issues squarely. He will make the kind of forthright hard-hitting campaign that American voters admire. This is why he is the man the left-leaning liberals most fear. He is the only Republican who will truly offer the voters "a choice, not an echo".

As Goldwater's grassroots strength grew in 1963 and early 1964, the leftwing propaganda against him grew in geometric proportion. LIFE Magazine put into words an anti-Goldwater argument that has appeared in one form or another in numerous magazines and newspaper columns. LIFE said we must beware of Goldwater because he has one-sentence solutions for national problems. According to this peculiar line of egghead reasoning, present day problems are so complex that we must have sophisticated — not simple — solutions.

Contrary to this argument, civilization progresses, freedom is won, and problems are solved because we have wonderful people who think up simple solutions! It is not the complicated, roundabout Rube Goldberg approach that accomplishes anything, but the direct approach that goes to the heart of the problem.

The man who did as much as anyone to emancipate women from their daily drudgery was the inventor of the sewing machine. His invention depended on a very simple idea; just put the eye of the needle in the point instead of in the other end.

Two brothers named Wright who ran a bicycle shop in Dayton, Ohio, had the ambition to invent an airplane. They received long letters from experts at the Smithsonian Institution and from Professors at European universities telling them that heavier-than-air flight was impossible. But the Wright brothers had two simple solutions — the curved wing to provide lift, and the propeller — and with these simple solutions, they built and flew the first airplane. Their simple solutions dominated air travel until the perfection of the jet engine.

When our infant Republic was threatened by the greatest military conquerer of the 19th century, our Minister to France said: "Millions for defense sir, but not one cent for tribute." This simple solution brought peace, not war.

When an American citizen named Perdicaris was captured and held hostage by a bandit named Raisuli, President Theodore Roosevelt had a simple solution: just send a cable reading "Perdicaris alive or Raisuli dead." It got results; Perdicaris was promptly released. Today, American servicemen are held hostage by Red bandits from East Germany to Cuba, to Red China, and no one has tried to get them out by simple solutions.

In 1958 the Chinese Reds made their big drive to take over Quemoy and Matsu. Appeasement-minded pundits at home urged that we evacuate these islands because "Why die for Quemoy?" President Eisenhower had a simple solution: he just went on television and told the world the United States would stand firm in the Formosa Straits. Shortly afterwards the Reds gave up their attacks, and for six years these islands have been secure outposts of freedom.

Likewise, there are numerous simple solutions for most of the problems that confront our country today. Barry Goldwater is the man who can cut through the egghead complexities in Foggy Bottom and solve these problems for us.

There is a very simple solution for what to do about Cuba — just reinstate the Monroe Doctrine. It would rid us of Castro and his subversion. We should not submit to the international blackmail of the false claim that using the Monroe Doctrine will start World War III. In 140 years of use, the Monroe Doctrine never brought war; it brought only peace. It would bring peace today if only we had a President with the courage to use it. Barry Goldwater is that man.

There was a very simple solution to what to do about the Berlin Wall. The Soviets started building it on Friday evening after our President had left Washington for a weekend holiday. By the time he returned to the White House on Monday afternoon, the Wall was built; the State Deparment wrung its hands and said: "There is nothing we can do now. What do you want to do, start World War III?" The solution was simple. A president with leadership could have made this announcement Friday night: "If the Communists close that door in Berlin, we will close the doors of the Soviet Embassy and consulates in our country." The Soviets would do anything to keep open these privileged sanctuaries which serve as the headquarters of their subversion, espionage and propaganda in the United States.

There was a very simple solution to what to do about the Congo: let the Congolese solve it! When they had a chance, they got rid of the Communist Lumumba. They would have eliminated the rest of the Communists, if our State Department had not, in collusion with the UN, told the Congolese they had to be more democratic and admit Communist followers of Lumumba into their government.

There is a simple solution as to what to do about Southeast Asia: just follow the advice of our greatest military authority on the Far East, General Douglas MacArthur. He said that Red China's aggressions could be stopped by announcing the end of the privileged Red sanctuaries requested by Attlee, granted by Acheson and still respected. General MacArthur thought it was wrong to send American boys to die in Asia, while refusing to use any of the 600,000 trained soldiers of the Republic of China or other means available for victory.

There is a very simple solution to what to do about the problem of world Communism: just stop helping the Communists. The Soviet empire would die of its own economic anemia if Democratic Administrations didn't keep giving it massive blood transfusions, such as the sending of 64 million bushels of American wheat.

There is a very simple solution to the problem

of peace and disarmament. It was given to us by the Father of Our Country, George Washington. The formula is as good today as when he said it: "If we desire to secure peace . . . it must be known that we are at all times ready for war."

Finally, there is a very simple solution to what to do about the whole "looney" mess in Washington today — elect Barry Goldwater, the man with the courage to give us simple solutions.

Chapter Twelve

Anybody But Goldwater

After Barry Goldwater announced his candidacy, the big question was: Where did the secret kingmakers fit into the 1964 picture? Would they say: "We picked the Republican nominee at each of the last seven conventions, so it is only fair to let someone else have a chance?" Would the kingmakers concede: "We had New Yorker Wendell Willkie in 1940, New Yorker Tom Dewey in 1944 and 1948, New Yorker Dwight Eisenhower in 1952 and 1956, and Richard Nixon who is now a New Yorker in 1960—and it is time for one of the other 49 states to name the nominee?" Would the kingmakers admit: "Goldwater is the obvious choice, so we'll sit this one out?"

Anyone who thought these things was quickly brought to reality in 1964. The kingmakers recognized Goldwater as a Republican they could not control. They started from the premise that the Republican Convention must nominate *anybody* but Goldwater.

The chief propaganda organ of the secret kingmakers, THE NEW YORK TIMES, revealed this drive for anybody but Goldwater in a surprisingly candid article bylined by one of its Washington correspondents, Tom Wicker. This report said:

The most bitter resistance to Senator Goldwater centers in the "eastern, internationalist power structure that for two decades has dictated Republican nominations. The members of that elite will not lightly relinquish their party to Barry Goldwater."[1]

Popular national magazines goosestepped for this "internationalist power structure" by featuring anti-Goldwater articles. The November 2, 1963 issue of THE NEW YORKER, a slick sophisticated magazine beamed to the carriage trade, sandwiched a profile on Goldwater amid 200 pages of luxury advertising. The author was Richard Rovere, a former editor of the Communist magazine NEW MASSES. NEWSWEEK Magazine of November 4, 1963 featured a byline column called "The Odds Against Goldwater" by Emmet John Hughes, who turned out a neat, but false, phrase, and said that Goldwater would not win because "he had yet — seriously — to face his foes . . . to face his friends . . . to face the issues. The fact is that no politician in either party has made his position as clear as has Goldwater, who has written two books defining his position on all major issues.

THE SATURDAY EVENING POST of January 25, 1964, featured an article called "How the Republicans Can Win" by Arthur Larson, the originator of the term "modern Republicanism." Larson, who never won an election, advised the GOP that it could win only if it appealed to the "Authentic American Center".

When he proceeded to define where this is, the only recent prominent figure he could think of who occupied the "Center" was President Kennedy who, like President Johnson, was recorded as voting conservative on only 10% of his Senate votes.

Behind the scenes, the kingmakers prepared the publicity buildup of several candidates to replace Barry Goldwater. How can the average person spot the kingmakers' candidates? Here is a sure litmus-paper test:

1. A kingmaker candidate does not criticize other kingmaker candidates.
2. Kingmaker candidates criticize Senator Goldwater more than they criticize Lyndon Johnson.
3. Kingmaker candidates never criticize the Democratic foreign giveaway programs.
4. Kingmaker candidates never criticize the State Department or the concessions it has made to the Communist axis.
5. Kingmaker candidates hardly ever raise the issue of Communism, either foreign or domestic.

The first choice of the kingmakers was Nelson Rockefeller. Who else but Nels? But Rockefeller chose a second wife rather than a second chance at the presidency. He remained in the race on the off-hand chance that he might, by some stroke of luck, win the crown; but primarily his function was to be a "spoiler". The kingmakers used Rockefeller to make a direct attack on Goldwater, so that, as we went into the stretch, the word could be passed down from on high that "Goldwater and Rockefeller have both made so many enemies that what we need is a compromise candidate who will be acceptable to both sides."

Rockefeller candidly admitted that when he was "the frontrunner, as I was, it's natural to try to unite all wings of the party," but after Goldwater forged ahead, "I'm off the unity kick." His name-calling blasts at Goldwater included such intemperate language as "ruthless, roughshod intimidation . . . cynical expediency . . . betrayal of principles."[2]

The second prong of the assault against Goldwater was to encourage state delegations pledged to favorite sons so that deals could be made at the opportune moment. Meanwhile the kingmakers engaged in a frantic search to dig up anybody — just anybody — to prevent Republicans from selecting their obvious candidate.

About once a month, some spokesman for the kingmakers sent up a trial balloon to test public reaction to a new candidate. In 1963 a trial balloon was sent up for General Lauris Norstad. He is very handsome and has a fine head of hair which, while Kennedy was President, seemed to be important qualifications.

Next came a boomlet for George Romney, Governor of Michigan. Like Rockefeller, and unlike Goldwater or Lyndon Johnson, Romney is handicapped by the absence of World War II military service. Even after he was dropped by the kingmakers, Romney was faithful to their wishes. On June 7, he violated his long standing rule against politicking on Sunday to announce: "I will do everything within my power to prevent him (Goldwater) from becoming the party's presidential choice."

One day in early 1964, a reporter asked Richard Nixon who he thought the next Republican nominee would be. Nixon replied that there were three strong candidates: Nelson Rockefeller, Barry Goldwater and Lucius Clay. The inclusion of Lucius Clay came as quite a surprise to rank-and-file Republicans. Why did Lucius Clay rate mention as one of the three top candidates? Clay is one of the inner clique of secret kingmakers, and Nixon, allowing himself to be used as a spokesman, was sending up a trial balloon.

As the Convention approached, the kingmakers had almost exhausted their list of "stop Goldwater" candidates: Harold Stassen, who hasn't been elected in more than 20 years; Henry Cabot Lodge, Lyndon Johnson's Ambassador to South Viet Nam, who was last elected to office in 1946, and who has since suffered two major defeats; and Richard Nixon, who abandoned California after his defeat for Governor and moved into an apartment building in New York owned and occupied by Nelson Rockefeller.

The kingmakers realized the crucial nature of the California primary on June 2 and threw their vast financial and propaganda apparatus behind Nelson Rockefeller. The San Francisco

and Los Angeles newspapers, LOOK, NEWS-
WEEK, TIME and LIFE magazines, the
columnists and commentators, the pollsters, etc.,
all attacked Goldwater in every conceivable
manner. Goldwater's victory proved that even
a fortune in paid workers and hidden persuaders
could not match the tens of thousands of dedicated volunteer grassroots workers who didn't
stop until the ballots were counted.

Remaining after California was only William
W. Scranton, Governor of Pennsylvania. Until
the stimulated publicity started in early 1964,
Scranton was unknown in national affairs. His
entire political experience consisted of one term
in the House of Representatives and one year
as Governor.

Four different groups of well-placed individuals in Harrisburg, in Philadelphia, in New
York, and elsewhere in the Northeast had worked
individually and in concert to promote Scranton as a presidential candidate. While the average citizen could detect no formal coordination
among them, there was no working at cross-pur-
poses, and they all acted with Scranton's knowledge. Here are the four developments.[3]

In Philadelphia, the kingmakers conducted
a careful project of "exposure" — showing off
Scranton to leading banking, industrial and communications figures in a series of private luncheons. The current representative of the Morgan
Guaranty Trust Company of New York is its

President, Thomas S. Gates, former secretary of
Defense. Gates of Morgan Guaranty is the king-
maker successor of Thomas Lamont of J. P.
Morgan and Company who masterminded the
Willkie blitz.

The host of these exclusive luncheons was Thomas B. McCabe, president of Scott Paper Company and, more importantly, former chairman of
the Board of Governors of the Federal Reserve
System and Public Governor of the New York
Stock Exchange.

The McCabe luncheons exposed Governor Scranton both to potential big money contributors and to key individuals in the communications field. Among the key industrialists and
news media persuaders who attended these
luncheons were former Secretary of Defense Neil
McElroy, now chairman of the Proctor and Gam-
ble Soap empire; Walter Thayer, former counsel
of the Citizens for Eisenhower and now president of the NEW YORK HERALD TRIB-
UNE; Arthur W. Dean, senior partner in the
largest New York law firm, Sullivan and Crom-
well; David Kendall, former White House counsel, now a Chrysler corporation vice president;
and James Hagerty, Eisenhower's press secretary and now an American Broadcasting Company vice president, in which capacity he defended the television attack on Richard Nixon by
Alger Hiss on Veteran's Day, 1962.

The money and publicity potential of these
luncheons was more than adequate to launch

Scranton full-blown as a presidental candidate.
The guest list at these luncheons included many
of the important financial contacts McCabe has
made in 47 years as a businessman and banker,
all potential contributors when the time became
ripe. Thomas S. Gates had also helped lay the financial groundwork with his important contractors
and with bankers and businessmen in Philadelphia
and New York. Scranton himself has an estimat-
ed $9,000,000 fortune, enough to make a consid-
erable contribution to the pre-Convention effort.

In Harrisburg, Scranton's hand-picked Republican State Chairman, Craig Truax, and other
Pennsylvania Republican officials worked to soft-
sell out-of-state Republicans on Scranton as the
man who could bind up the GOP wounds ex-
pected from the Rockefeller-Goldwater pre-Convention battle. Truax suggested to Goldwater
supporters in the south and elsewhere that Scranton would be their best alternative if Goldwater
did not get the nomination.

In New York, a young lawyer named Warren
J. Sinsheimer launched a "Draft Scranton"
campaign in the pattern of the popular petition
effort for Wendell Willkie in 1940. Sinsheimer
conferred with close Scranton political con-
fidants and, while he was given no official
approval, neither was he told to stop.

It is significant that Draft Scranton petitions
carried the following wording at the top:

> "The undersigned urge Governor William
> Scranton of Pennsylvania to seek actively

the 1964 Republican Presidential Nomination. *Regardless of political affiliation,* we
the undersigned urge that he be nominated for President at the Republican National Convention." (emphasis added)[4]

In other words, as in 1940 and especially in
1952, the kingmakers urged non-Republicans
to come over and help prevent the Republican
National Convention from nominating its obvious first choice.

In the communications media, the publicity
blitz was given the GO signal. As one newspap-
erman put it, suddenly "Governor Scranton has
become hot copy." National reporters began running in and out of Harrisburg at an unprecedented pace, and competing news organizations
scrambled to keep pace. The NEW YORK
HERALD TRIBUNE led off with an editorial
titled "Calling Governor Scranton". Stewart Al-
sop, an ADA founder, was the author of a feature article in the SATURDAY EVENING
POST called "The Logical Candidate". THE
NEW YORK TIMES MAGAZINE gave large
space to favorable portrayals of Scranton. The
WALL STREET JOURNAL joined the cabal
and called Scranton "the betting favorite among
some of the most knowledgeable GOP leaders".
Walter Lippmann advised Republicans to nominate Scranton even though conceding that Scranton had little prospect of defeating Johnson.

Scranton was the subject of a friendly cover story in NEWSWEEK. LOOK had a flat-
tering article and the READER'S DIGEST

joined in with six pages of fulsome praise. Scranton was featured in FORTUNE in a long story about his state industrial development. LIFE Magazine highlighted a lengthy profile by Theodore H. White, author of the prize-winning book about President Kennedy. The Luce publications have always been part of the kingmaking establishment. It certainly is no handicap to Scranton that his brother-in-law, James A. Linen, is President of TIME.

The ST. LOUIS GLOBE-DEMOCRAT predicted that when all these developments are

> "pulled together and coordinated by men who know how nominees are made, they provide all the basic ingredients — money publicity, party support, seasoned political leadership and popular grass roots activity — to make a presidential candidate."[5]

After saying he would accept only a "genuine draft that is not engineered", — which never developed — Scranton drafted himself just one month before the Convention opened.

Chapter Thirteen

Victory For The Grassroots

1964

Governor Scranton started on the campaign trail by announcing that his hope of winning the nomination lay in taking some 200 "moveable" Delegates from Barry Goldwater's announced pledges of more than 600. Immediately the kingmakers' immense financial and propaganda apparatus went into high gear to sell Scranton to Republicans. His every ghost-written word became front-page copy, with ghostwriters Malcolm Moos and William Keisling scripting Goldwater as the villain instead of LBJ. The other kingmaker candidates closed ranks behind Scranton; Henry Cabot Lodge rushed home from South Viet Nam to jump on the Scranton bandwagon. As the kingmakers twisted the arm of our communications media, Scranton began a meteoric rise on that adjustable thermometer of kingmaker hopes, the Gallup Poll.

As the Delegates gathered in San Francisco for the 1964 Republican National Convention, the kingmakers trotted out all their tried-and-true tactics of previous Conventions. A veteran journalist, personally opposed to Goldwater and writing for an anti-Goldwater newspaper, described this onslaught:

"An attack upon Goldwater of a ferocity never remotely approached in any of the eight national party conventions previously attended by this columnist was then opened . . . They, the 'moderns', loosed upon Goldwater a storm of accusation and innuendo that made their assaults upon the late Senator Robert A. Taft in 1952 look like warm endorsements. Men of the stature of Nelson Rockefeller and Henry Cabot Lodge appeared before 40,000 Negro demonstrators in the streets in open incitation of them against the candidacy of the man about to be chosen to head their own party, Goldwater.

"Scranton camp followers spread shocking tales suggesting that Goldwater was perhaps in league with neo-Nazis in Germany — and this about a man whose own father was Jewish. Scranton himself attacked Goldwater, in his challenge to a 'debate', in tones plainly implying that Goldwater was not only wrong but actually evil."[1]

These tactics were not successful because in 1964 the majority of Convention Delegates were independent citizens elected in their districts who sought — not personal advancement or political jobs — but only the nomination and election of a candidate who would end the America Last policies of the past 30 years.

On July 12 the kingmakers released their contrived Gallup and Harris polls. The latter falsely described the Goldwater position as favoring "Go to war over Cuba," "Using A-bombs in

Asia," and "Against social security." The un-
scientific nature of many polls was revealed
by Marvin D. Field, formerly with the Gallup
poll and now head of one of the polls which
picked Rockefeller to beat Goldwater in the
California primary, who admitted to the press
that he polled only 256 out of 3,002,038 registered Republicans in California. He thus based his prediction on .000085 of Republican voters.[2]

As a result of a luncheon strategy conference
on July 12 with Rockefeller and Lodge, Scranton caused to be drafted and released that evening his letter which charged that Goldwater
had "bought, beaten and compromised" the
Delegates. This was a revealing admission from
the kingmakers that they thought the 1964 Republican Delegates could be "bought" and "compromised."

As the Convention opened on July 13, the
final strategy of the kingmakers was to harass
and delay the Convention by raising phony issues in the hope that a miracle would happen.
Each day Henry Cabot Lodge (referred to at
the Cow Palace as Henry Sabotage) announced
we could expect a "surprise" or a "bombshell."
The kingmaker forces waged a tedious struggle
in the Rules Committee and also in the Credentials Committee where they tried to raise the
spurious issues of race, but were able to muster
only 19 votes out of 100.

On July 14 Nelson Rockefeller and George

Romney demanded that the Republican Platform be amended to include an anti-extremism plank. They denounced some Goldwater supporters as extremists, but were unwilling to denounce such radical societies as Cosa Nostra, the Black Muslims, CORE (which was then engaged in civil disobedience and lie-ins at the Cow Palace), the Fair Play for Cuba Committee (one of whose members assassinated President Kennedy), the hundreds of Communist fronts on the Attorney General's list; or radical left-wing societies influential in the Democratic Party such as the Americans for Democratic Action and the Ad Hoc Committee for the Triple Revolution. The hypocrisy of these amendments was clear to the Delegates who overwhelmingly voted them down.

Rockefeller complained that his speech was interrupted by the Delegates. As long as he confined himself to the subject, he was given quiet attention. But the California Delegates knew he had conducted a rough no-holds-barred campaign against Goldwater in their state and had mailed out a million reprints of LOOK Magazine's smear on Goldwater. When Rockefeller insinuated that Goldwater supporters used "Communist and Nazi methods" and cited the cancellation of his political appearance at a University in Los Angeles (Loyola, for reasons it considered proper), the California Delegates voiced disapproval of his smear. As John L. Lewis said in explaining his fisticuffs with Bill Hutcheson at an

AFL Convention, when an honorable man is called a bad name, he must either pretend he didn't hear, or express righteous indignation. California heard because it was the closest delegation to Rocky's rostrum.

The next ploy of the kingmakers was to demand a platform amendment that the President alone should be able to decide on the use of atomic weapons. This was asking the Delegates to deny a Republican President the power of deputizing use of atomic weapons which Republicans had entrusted to Democrats Kennedy and Johnson. If, as in 1919 and 1955, the President were stricken for months by a severe heart attack, no one would be authorized to defend our country with nuclear weapons. This kingmaker stratagem was defeated two to one.

The communications media overdid itself in carrying out the directives of the kingmakers to attack Goldwater. On July 16 Senator Goldwater said: "Newspapers like the NEW YORK TIMES have to stoop to utter dishonesty in reflecting my views. Some of the newspapers here in San Francisco like the CHRONICLE . . . are nothing but out and out lies." He said a CBS broadcast by Daniel Schorr that Goldwater was going to Munich to start his campaign where the fuehrer (Hitler) started his campaign was a "dirty lie."[3] Even the mild-mannered Dwight Eisenhower advised the Delegates:

"Let us particularly scorn the divisive efforts of those outside our family, includ-

ing sensation-seeking columnists and commentators, because my friends these are
people who couldn't care less about the
good of our party."

Republicans will be foolishly naive if they
think the defeated kingmakers will now give
Goldwater the same party loyalty that conserva-
tives have given them for the past 28 years.
While some may give lip service to Goldwater's
campaign, realism requires us to anticipate that
the kingmakers will use their immense financial
and propaganda apparatus in behalf of the reelection of Lyndon Johnson.

TIME Magazine laid down the line on May
22: "A lot of the kingmakers think that President Johnson, all things being relative, has done
a good job." Walter Lippmann expanded on this
when he said on May 26 that "the old established
ruling powers in the Republican Party— the
banking, industrial, and publishing magnates in
the large metropolitan centers — are either in
favor of the election of President Johnson or at
least are not strongly opposed to it." Henry
Ford II, who never before voted for any Democrat for president, announced that he would support and vote for President Johnson in the 1964
election because "he's terrific" and "an awful
lot of business people are for President Johnson."[4]

Chapter Fourteen

Who are the Secret Kingmakers?

Several questions naturally arise: Can it really be possible that a little clique of powerful men meet secretly and plan events that appear to "just happen"? Who are the secret kingmakers who manipulated and controlled Republican National Conventions from 1936 through 1960? What is their motive for exercising such control, even when it means the defeat of the Party they profess to serve? These are questions to be answered in this chapter.

The rational citizen believes in the principle of causality, that for every effect there must be a cause. Most of what is ascribed to "accident" or "coincidence" is really the result of human plans. When there is an airplane accident, the authorities make a diligent search for the series of events that led to the crash — and usually the cause is found.

Abraham Lincoln explained causal relationship in his "House Divided" speech:

> "But when we see a lot of framed timber, different portions of which we know have been gotten out at different times and places and by different workmen . . . and when we see these timbers joined together, and see they exactly make the frame of a house or a mill, all the tenons and mortises exactly fitting, . . . in such a case, we

find it impossible not to believe that . . . all understood one another from the beginning, and all worked upon a common plan."

Several years ago, the author of this book stumbled on clear evidence that very powerful men actually do meet to make plans which are kept secret from American citizens. While visiting at Sea Island, Georgia, this writer discovered the details of a secret meeting on nearby St. Simon's Island, Georgia, held at the King and Prince Hotel, February 14-18, 1957.

The most elaborate precautions were taken to prevent Americans from knowing who attended this secret meeting or what transpired there. Advance agents came in four months ahead to check security and search every room in the hotel. All hotel employees were given the most rigid security check and their names sent to Washington for additional investigation. During the four days and five nights of the meeting, all roads leading to the hotel were blocked off and the road block maintained by the Georgia State Police. The hotel was closed to all other patrons. NATO and FBI guards in plain clothes kept constant surveillance on the hotel itself.

None of the hotel employees was permitted to go into the ballroom where the meetings were held. At the end of each session, one of the participants personally gathered up all notes and memos used during the meeting and burned them.

Who were the participants at this secret meeting at St. Simon's Island? They were many of the top-level kingmakers who exercise financial, political and propaganda control over American citizens and policies. The 69 participants on the official unpublished list included the following:

George W. Ball, now Undersecretary of State in the Johnson Administration,

Eugene R. Black, then President of the International Bank for Reconstruction and Development,

McGeorge Bundy, now top presidential adviser on security in the Johnson Administration,

Arthur H. Dean, disarmament negotiator for the State Department under Republican and Democrat administrations,

Thomas E. Dewey, twice Republican presidential candidate,

J. William Fulbright, Senator from Arkansas, later author of the Fulbright Memorandum, a directive to muzzle our military, who on March 25, 1964 called on the United States to "accept Red Cuba",

Paul G. Hoffman, former U.S. Chief of all foreign aid,

C. D. Jackson, vice president of TIME, Inc.,

Per Jacobsen, Managing Director, World Monetary Fund,

George F. Kennan, Ambassador to the Soviet Union, and later chief advisor on Communism to the Kennedy Administration,

Ralph E. McGill, Editor, ATLANTA CONSTITUTION,

Paul H. Nitze, later Secretary of the Navy in the Johnson Administration,

David Rockefeller, now president of the Chase Manhattan Bank,

Dean Rusk, now Secretary of State,

Arthur Hays Sulzberger, president and publisher of the NEW YORK TIMES,

Alexander Wiley, Republican Senator from Wisconsin and senior Republican on the Senate Foreign Relations Committee.

President Eisenhower was at the Augusta National Golf Club during this meeting. Tom Dewey kept in touch with him from the telephone in the bar at the King and Prince Hotel. Other kingmakers who kept in touch with the meeting and who may have been present part of the time include Nelson Rockefeller, Harold Stassen, Thomas S. Lamont, Dean Acheson, Gardner Cowles, Winthrop Aldrich and Walter Lippmann.

The participants at the St. Simon's meeting were some of the biggest names in American politics, business and the press. As described by an eye-witness observer of that meeting, "Those who came were not the heads of states, but those who give orders to heads of states," — in other words, the kingmakers. Who was there, who got this priceless collection of prominent people together under one roof, and what they discussed and decided — should have been front-page news on every newspaper in America. These facts are interesting and important to all informed citizens.

But, no enterprising reporters covered this meeting of VIPs. Although three of the leading newsmen in America were present, Arthur Sulzberger of the NEW YORK TIMES, Ralph McGill of the ATLANTA CONSTITUTION, and C. D. Jackson of TIME, they did not print a word about this sensational meeting in their publications.

Other never-before-published details of this secret meeting make fascinating reading, even at this late date. Officially called DeBilderberg group, the U. S. kingmakers were joined on St. Simon's Island by a similarly select assortment of foreigners with whom financial and political contacts are maintained. The titular head of this secret group was Prince Bernhard of the Netherlands. The meeting was conducted with multilingual phones just like at the United Nations; one could merely push a button and get French, German or English from expert translators.

All participants arrived by corporate or private planes at the St. Simon's airport. The food was flown in from the Pierre Hotel in New York except for one seafood dinner prepared by the King and Prince Hotel. A wine list was prepared and printed especially for the meeting, with fine wines imported directly from France. The bill for the entire meeting was paid by H. J. Heinz II, President of the H. J. Heinz Company, except that David Rockefeller signed many of the bar checks. Nobody else was allowed to pay for anything.

DeBilderbergers have met once or twice a year since their first meeting at DeBilderberg Hotel in the Netherlands in May 1954. Their most recent meeting was held March 20-22, 1964, at the Rockefeller restoration at Williamsburg, Virginia.

Leading these deliberations were prominent leftwing Democrats such as UnderSecretary of State George W. Ball and former Secretary of State Dean Acheson who said after Hiss' conviction: "I will not turn my back on Alger Hiss." Like-minded foreign politicians present included Prime Minister Lester Pearson of Canada. The meetings were closed and no reports were given to the press.

The St. Simon's meeting of DeBilderbergers holds several important lessons for Americans today.

(1) It proves that there do in fact exist secret groups of persons high in finance, government and the press who meet secretly to make important plans they do not reveal to the public. DeBilderbergers is only one of these groups.

(2) It shows that these secret meetings are heavily weighted in favor of the liberal foreign viewpoint and loaded with Americans who have important financial and business contacts and investments abroad — to the exclusion of persons with a pro-American viewpoint.

(3) It shows that Republicans are in a small minority in these meetings, and are always of the liberal "me too" variety.

(4) It shows that the top level "me too" Republicans have a close social, business and political working relationship with top-level leftwing Democrats.

Highly placed New York kingmakers work toward "convergence" between the Republican and Democratic parties so as to preserve their America Last foreign policy and eliminate foreign policy from political campaigns.

The secret kingmakers exercise their influence in both parties. In 1932 the New York kingmakers were confident that, because of the depression, whoever won the Democratic nomination, would be the next President. Their New York candidate was opposed by two Presidential candidates who could not be controlled, Alfred E. Smith and Senator James Reed of Missouri. So the kingmakers made a deal with the leader of the most ruthless political machine in America, Huey Long. The New York kingmakers said that they would vote to seat Huey Long and his followers as Delegates from Louisiana, although the Convention Credentials Committee had approved the anti-Long Delegates. In exchange, Huey Long helped round up enough votes to nominate Franklin D. Roosevelt.

It is easy to spot the most trusted agents of the kingmakers because they are men who move with ease in and out of both parties. They appear to have a magic ability to be named to top government positions by both Republicans and Democrats. Here are a few examples:

Nelson Rockefeller, Coordinator of Latin American Affairs for the Roosevelt Administration, and Republican candidate for president in 1964.

Henry Cabot Lodge, Ambassador to South Viet Nam for the Kennedy and Johnson Administrations, and Republican candidate for president in 1964.

Robert Strange McNamara, a man who called himself a Republican, but who served as Secretary of Defense for the Kennedy and the Johnson Administrations.

C. Douglas Dillon, Undersecretary of State for the Eisenhower Administration, who mysteriously was carried over as Secretary of the Treasury for the Kennedy and the Johnson Administrations.

Arthur H. Dean, chief negotiator at Panmunjom for the Eisenhower Administration, who carried over as disarmament adviser for the Kennedy Administration.

Paul G. Hoffman, "modern Republican", who served as foreign aid head for the Truman Administration, and then was named Manager of the UN Special Fund by the Eisenhower Administration.

Robert B. Anderson, who served as Secretary of the Navy and then Secretary of the Treasury under the Eisenhower Administration, is now L.B.J.'s "special ambassador to work out a settlement with Panama."

For highly-placed Republicans to accept appointments from the Democrats is destructive of the two-party system. The voters expect Republicans to be Republicans, and Democrats to be Democrats. Trading in and out of both parties confuses the issues and especially the responsibility — which is indeed the motive of the kingmakers who direct this traffic as easily as an expert playing chess.

This is also a technique which has been used by Democrats to undercut Republican opposition to Democrat policies. In 1940 during the Republican National Convention, when Roosevelt's war intervention policy was the major issue, Roosevelt boldly appointed two prominent Republicans to his Cabinet: Henry L. Stimson as Secretary of War and Frank Knox as Secretary of the Navy. This was a clever move of the master politician to divide and confuse Republicans, and to prevent them from making his war policy the campaign it should have been.

Later when Roosevelt extended favors to Wendell Willkie and sent him around the world on a U.S. Government bomber with an Air Force crew, this was a move designed to soften Republican opposition to Roosevelt's "grand design to appease Stalin," and it achieved considerable success.

Likewise today, President Johnson is cleverly using Republicans to cover his most controversial policies and prevent them from being issues in the 1964 campaign.

He is using Secretary of Defense Robert Mc-

Namara, a Republican, to camouflage the tragic disarmament policies of the Johnson Administration, the cancellation of such strategic weapons as the Skybolt, the RS-70, the Pluto nuclear missile, and the Nike-Zeus, and the closing down of our missile bases in Turkey and Italy.

President Johnson is using Republican C. Douglas Dillon as Secretary of the Treasury to front for the $100 billion budget, the largest peacetime budget in our history.

President Johnson is using Henry Cabot Lodge, Republican vice presidential candidate in 1960, to cover for the Administration's sellout to the Communists in South Viet Nam. Viet Nam should be as important and winning an issue for Republicans in 1964 as Korea was in 1952. But Republicans are handicapped from making it a campaign issue because of Henry Cabot Lodge's complicity in the tragic blunders.

Among the most influential kingmakers who profess to be Republicans is the Morgan banking group headed by Thomas S. Lamont, Jr., son of the Thomas S. Lamont who masterminded Willkie's nomination, and brother of Corliss Lamont, a leading Soviet apologist. Thomas S. Gates, the present president of Morgan Guaranty Trust Company, is the son of Thomas S. Gates, who installed Harold Stassen as President of the University of Pennsylvania in 1948.

Other New York kingmakers active in perpetuating the foreign giveaway programs which have so completely failed to stop Communism

are the Averell Harriman group, which controls
Brown Brothers Harriman and Company; the
Rockefeller group, which controls New York's
two largest banks, the Chase Manhattan Bank
and the First National City Bank and which
interlocks with the Morgan group through joint
directors; the Whitney-Reid group which controls
the NEW YORK HERALD TRIBUNE and
its anti-Goldwater syndicated columnist Walter
Lippmann; the Eugene Meyer group which controls the WASHINGTON POST and NEWS-
WEEK; the Gardner Cowles group, which controls LOOK Magazine, the MINNEAPOLIS
STAR, and the DES MOINES REGISTER;
the Henry Luce group which controls TIME,
LIFE, and FORTUNE and published the "Big
Steal" attack on Senator Taft in 1952 two days
ahead of TIME'S regular issue day so as to have
maximum effect on the Republican Convention
Delegates.

On May 18, 1964, NEWSWEEK printed pictures of some of the upper echelon kingmakers
determined to stop Goldwater: General Lucius
Clay of Lehman Bros., former Secretary of Defense Thomas S. Gates, president of Morgan
Guaranty Trust Co., investment banker Sidney
J. Weinberg, and Gardner Cowles publisher of
LOOK which provided the principal campaign
piece for Rockefeller's California campaign.

The New York kingmakers' establishment in-
cludes all those financial leaders who favor a
continuation of the Roosevelt - Harry Dexter

White - Averell Harriman - Dean Acheson - Dean Rusk policy of *aiding* and *abetting* Red Russia and her satellites. These financiers, some of whom profess to be Republicans, have never criticized the following Democrat policies:

1) Recognizing Red Russia after three Republican Presidents refused to do so;

2) Overlooking Red Russia's violation of the Litvinov-Roosevelt agreement to permit religious freedom in Russia and to refrain from propaganda and espionage in the United States;

3) Overlooking Red Russia's failure to pay its World War I and World War II debts to us of $12,351,952,530, its post World War II debt to us of $500,000,000, and its seizure without compensation of America private property worth billions in Iron Curtain countries;

4) Condoning Red Russia's invasion of its peaceful neighbors: Finland, Latvia, Lithuania, Estonia, Poland, Czechoslovakia, Hungary, etc.;

5) Giving to Red Russia at Teheran, Yalta and Potsdam control of Eastern Europe, Manchuria, North Korea, the Kurile Islands, all World War II anti-Communist Russian refugees, plus three votes in the UN;

6) Letting China fall to the Communists under the Lattimore-Acheson-Institute of Pacific Relations policies;

7) Continuing to send billions of American dollars to Communists such as Tito who still proclaims, "I am a Communist and nothing but a Communist,"[1] and to Sukarno who told the

U.S. to "go to hell with your aid";[2]

8) Accepting the continued violation of the Monroe Doctrine in Cuba;

9) Delivering U.S. wheat to Red Russia and its agents, such as the Continental Grain Company owned by French banking interests, at prices far below the cost of production and shipping.

What is the motive of the secret kingmakers?

During the Roosevelt Administration, their chief motive was surreptitiously to get the American taxpayers to protect the kingmakers' heavy investments in England and Western Europe.

Since the end of World War II, the United States foreign giveaway programs have become immensely profitable for certain Americans.

From July 1, 1946 to June 30, 1963, the U.S. gave away abroad $148,456,330,000. This is $46.7 billion *more* than the total assessed valuation of America's 50 largest cities. There are large profits to be made in acting as depositary, or fiscal agent, or issuer of letters of credit, or purchasing agent, or attorney for the foreign recipients of these immense sums, or as broker for the seller of goods purchased under the foreign aid program, both here and abroad.

The New York kingmakers, for pocketbook reasons, are extremely anxious to prevent any curtailment of the foreign giveaway program. This might come about:

1) by the election of a president who did *not* put the welfare of America secondary to the welfare of every other country from Albania

to Zanzibar, or

2) by the collapse of the Communist system which is the sole excuse for the foreign aid program.

Voltaire once said: "If there were no God, it would be necessary to invent Him." Time and time again, the Communist regime has been saved from collapse by American diplomatic, military or economic assistance — under the America Last foreign policy dictated by the kingmakers: in 1933 when Roosevelt recognized the Soviet Union just after the food shortages and revolts caused by the liquidation of the kulaks; in 1941-42 during the Hitler-Stalin struggle; in 1953 when Stalin died; in 1956 when the Hungarian Freedom Fighters threw off the Soviet yoke in Hungary and could have touched off a wave of revolts behind the Iron Curtain; and again in 1962-64 when Red China and the Soviet Union ran out of food.

This hidden policy of perpetuating the Red empire in order to perpetuate the high level of Federal spending and control is revealed in secret studies made by the Kennedy Administration.[3]

The kingmakers have a vested interest in preventing — at all cost — the election of a president such as Barry Goldwater who will let the Soviet system collapse of its own internal weaknesses, who will curtail the foreign giveaway programs, as well as the level of Federal spending, and whose foreign policy will serve the best interests of the United States of America.

Also, the New York kingmakers are not opposed to the New Deal — New Frontier — Fast Deal policy of deficit financing which results in buying the people's votes with their own money. The national debt has been raised six times by the Democrats since 1961. Senator John J. Williams recently proved that Democratic administrations are responsible for $293 billion of the national debt while Republican administrations are chargeable with only $13 billion.

Since the New York kingmakers dominate the consortium which fixes the interest rate the Government has to pay on its obligations, they have no incentive to see deficit financing stop. They even favor the Democrat policy of giving foreigners the right to exchange their dollars for gold or silver, but of denying this right to American citizens. The only way to stop the spend and elect policy of LBJ, supported by the kingmakers and their lackeys, is to vote for candidates *not* controlled by the kingmakers.

Chapter Fifteen

Why This Book Was Written

Some Republicans may ask, why would a regular party Republican write a book which exposes the Convention intrigues of a few alleged Republicans? Should not the mistakes of our Conventions be discussed only in private? What useful purpose can be served by public discussion of our Convention shortcomings in a year when the survival of American freedom and independence may depend on a Republican victory which will turn out of office the ADA radicals in the White House, the unilateral disarmers in the Pentagon, and the "rather Red than dead" advocates in the State Department?

I have done volunteer work for the Republican Party ever since 1945. During those 19 years, I have given thousands and thousands of hours of dedicated work to the cause of good government through the medium of the Republican Party. I have traveled thousands of miles in order to speak to small groups and large, help little clubs, build stronger Republican organizations, inject enthusiasm, inspire and persuade women to work for the Party, and solve problems of many kinds.

I have done this at my own expense and at great sacrifice on my part and on the part of my family — for one purpose, because I believe in working for good government, and I believe this can be best achieved through the Republican Party. I have never sought to be appointed to any job on any level, or otherwise to gain material or personal advantage from my work for the Republican Party.

When the primary or the Republican National Convention did not nominate the candidate of my choice, I nevertheless stumped the state just as energetically and enthusiastically as when my favorites were selected.

I can look back on campaigns in which I saw Republicans on the local level working their hearts out for a cause they believed to be just, only to realize, after it was all over, that the kingmakers had given them a candidate who would not campaign on the issues. I speak with the voice of the countless Republican Party workers who don't want this to happen again; in the words of the greatest Republican slogan of this century, they have "had enough".

In the interest of Party unity, I kept silent as we sustained each tragic defeat. But as we started the crucial campaign of 1964, my loyalty to the thousands of Republicans who labor in the precincts compelled me to speak out. I believed it would have been dereliction of duty for me to fail to present the facts to our people so they could forestall another defeat like 1940, 1944, 1948 and 1960.

The decision to publish these pages was a hard one. The question was whether to try to help grassroots Republicans face the realities of 1964 politics, or whether to close my eyes, hope for the best, and run the grave risk of having to look into the eyes of hard-working Republicans in November, discouraged and disillusioned at another unnecessary defeat. I believed that the most constructive thing I could do for the Republican Party was to give our people the facts, in anticipation of the Convention, which would assist them to reject the efforts of the little clique of kingmakers who wanted to force upon us another "me too" candidate who would pull his punches and evade the vital issues. I made my decision in the light of what I believe to be the best interests of the America I love, the Republican Party I have served, and the voters to whom I owe a duty to speak the truth.

History shows that mistakes can be prevented by providing the people with facts and warnings in anticipation of a threatened event.

For example, on May 19, 1963 Republican Party Chairman William E. Miller gave public voice to persistent rumors that the State Department had made secret plans to appease Castro by turning over Guantanamo to him, and withdrawing American forces from Cuba to Puerto Rico. Because Miller revealed this in time with the appropriate publicity, the State Department did not have the nerve to consummate the "Guantanamo deal" it had hoped to slip through without the public realizing its significance. Miller halted the surrender of this important naval base for us by his advance warning.

Likewise, the nomination of Barry Goldwater by the 1964 Republican National Convention in San Francisco was a vivid demonstration of the axioms that "knowledge is power" and "to be forewarned is to be forearmed." Grassroots Republicans were on to the kingmakers' dirty tricks. Delegates were acutely aware of how the kingmakers had stolen previous Republican Conventions, and they were determined it would not happen again. Grassroots Republicans were fully prepared for the propaganda blitz, the vicious charges, the phony polls, the spurious issues, the slanted press — and they didn't crumble under the kingmakers' many-pronged attack.

Now that grassroots Republicans have succeeded in nominating Barry Goldwater and William E. Miller — two candidates who will campaign on the major issues of our time and fight hard to win — it has become more important than ever that this story be told to all voters, whether Republican, Democrat or Independent. Only in this way will the average voter be prepared for the propaganda onslaught that will be activated by the kingmakers against Goldwater. It will be massive and it will be clever. The kingmakers are playing for high stakes — control of Federal spending — and they do not intend to lose. Americans must learn the significance of these famous lines spoken by Patrick Henry in 1775:

"I have but one lamp by which my feet

are guided, and that is the lamp of experience. I know of no way of judging of
the future but by the past."

The burden for Goldwater's election will fall
on the same kind of dedicated volunteers who
won his nomination. The $100 billion question
is: Can grassroots Americans complete in November the victory they started winning in July?

REFERENCES

CHAPTER TWO

1 Associated Press Dispatch from Moscow, January 17, 1964

2 U.S. NEWS AND WORLD REPORT, December 27, 1957, p. 32.

3 WASHINGTON POST, July 6, 1960.

4 Associated Press Dispatch.

5 Ibid.

6 Released September 1961, Government Printing Office, Washington, D.C.

7 CONGRESSIONAL RECORD, June 19, 1962, p. 9966-8.

8 Special Report on the Phoenix Study, *U.S.A.* vol. 10, nos. 24, 25 and 26.

9 U.S. NEWS AND WORLD REPORT, January 27, 1964, p. 31.

10 Victor Riesel Column, January 20, 1964.

11 Associated Press Dispatch, January 17, 1964.

12 NEW YORK JOURNAL AMERICAN, March 2-5, 1964.

13 Allen-Scott Report, March 6, 1964.

14 U.S. NEWS AND WORLD REPORT, June 25, 1954, p. 79-80; also June 11, 1954, p. 82ff.

15 Doubleday and Co. v. New York, 335 U.S. 848, October 25, 1948.

16 THE COLD WAR AND THE INCOME TAX by Edmund Wilson, p. 115.

17 United Press Dispatch, August 30, 1963.

18 "Our Country's Inglorious Role in the Final Days of the Diem Regime" by Marguerite Higgins, HUMAN EVENTS, March 7, 1964, p. 8-9.

19 Allen-Scott Report, February 21, 1964.

CHAPTER THREE

1 HOW NOT TO RUN FOR PRESIDENT by James L. Wick, Vantage Press, Inc., New York, 1952, pp. 19-24.

2 CONGRESSIONAL RECORD, May 31, 1955, p A3761.

CHAPTER FOUR

1 Quoted in ONE MAN: WENDELL WILLKIE by C. Nelson Sparks, p. 5-7.

2 THE POLITICS OF UPHEAVAL by Arthur M. Schlesinger, Jr., Houghton Mifflin Co., Boston, 1960, p. 539.

3 Ibid, p. 533.

CHAPTER FIVE

1 WILLKIE by Joseph Barnes, Simon and Schuster, New York, 1952, p. 152.

2 THE REPUBLICAN PARTY AND WENDELL WILLKIE by Donald Bruce Jackson, University of Illinois Press, Urbana, 1960, p. 50.

3 Ibid, pp. 64-65.

4 CONGRESSIONAL RECORD, June 19, 1940, p. 12960.

5 Barnes, op. cit., p. 178.

6 Sparks, op. cit., p. 18.

7 Ibid, p. 20.

8 U.S. Senate Foreign Relations Committee Hearings, February 11, 1941.

CHAPTER SIX

1 THE WINNING SIDE by Ralph de Toledano, G. P. Putnam's Sons, New York, 1963, p. 84.

CHAPTER SEVEN

1 OUT OF THE JAWS OF VICTORY by Jules

Abels, Henry Holt and Company, New York, 1959, p. 63.

2 Wick, op. cit., Chapter 7.

3 ROLL CALL, October 26, 1960.

CHAPTER EIGHT

1 NATIONAL REVIEW, October 5, 1957, p. 295.

2 Speech at University of Pennsylvania, April 18, 1952.

3 July 5, 1952.

4 ELECTIONS 1964 by Edwin A. Roberts, Jr., Newsbook, the National Observer, Silver Spring, Maryland, 1964, p. 68.

5 Idem.

6 CHICAGO TRIBUNE, July 11, 1952.

7 NEW YORK TIMES, Nov. 25, 1959, p. 14.

8 AMERICAN BAR JOURNAL, Feb. 1958, p. 113-114, 192.

CHAPTER NINE

1 NEW YORK TIMES, July 24 and 31, 1956.

2 "The Stassen-Clay Plot That Failed" by Walter Trohan, HUMAN EVENTS, October 13, 1961, p. 679.

CHAPTER TEN

1 NEW YORK TIMES, July 25, 1960.

2 EAST ST. LOUIS JOURNAL, July 27, 1960.

3 NEWSWEEK, March 23, 1964, p. 24-25.

4 VIRGINIAN-PILOT, April 28, 1963, p. A-13.

CHAPTER TWELVE

1 "Anatomy of the Goldwater Boom" by Tom Wicker, NEW YORK TIMES MAGAZINE, August 11, 1963.

2 HUMAN EVENTS, August 3, 1963, p. 10.

3 "The Making of a Presidential Candidate" by Jules Witcover, ST. LOUIS GLOBE-DEMOCRAT, February 1-2, 1964; GOP's Political Pros Undecided as Amateurs Spotlight Governor Scranton" by Raymond P. Brandt, ST. LOUIS POST-DISPATCH, February 8, 1964; "GOP Old Pros Take Good Look at Scranton" by Rowland Evans and Robert Novak, ST. LOUIS POST-DISPATCH, January 21, 1964.

4 Petition distributed at Lincoln Day gathering of Missouri Republicans, Sheraton-Jefferson Hotel, St. Louis, Missouri, February 15, 1964.

5 ST. LOUIS GLOBE-DEMOCRAT, op. cit.

CHAPTER THIRTEEN

1 William S. White, LOS ANGELES TIMES, July 17, 1964.

2 CHICAGO TRIBUNE, May 29, 1964.

3 SAN FRANCISCO EXAMINER, July 18, 1964.

4 ST. LOUIS GLOBE-DEMOCRAT, May 23, 1964.

CHAPTER FOURTEEN

1 "Who Are They,", U.S. House Committee on Un-American Activities, October 17, 1957.

2 Associated Press Dispatch, March 26, 1964.

3 "A World Effectively Controlled by the UN", ARPA-IDA Study Memo No. 7, March 10, 1962, Dept. of State Contract SCC 28270, Feb. 24, 1961.

Cut Out and Mail

ORDER FORM

Pere Marquette Press,

P.O. Box 316, Alton, Illinois.

Send me .... copies of A CHOICE NOT AN ECHO

Payment of $............ is enclosed (send check or money order)

Name ....

Street ....

City and State ....

(Please Print)